W9-ADE-216

THE
WORLD'S
GREATEST
LOVE
LETTERS

COMPILED BY
MICHAEL KELAHAN

THE WORLD'S GREATEST LOVE LETTERS

FALL RIVER PRESS

New York

FALL RIVER PRESS

New York

An Imprint of Sterling Publishing
387 Park Avenue South
New York, NY 10016

FALL RIVER PRESS and the distinctive Fall River Press logo are registered
trademarks of Barnes & Noble, Inc.

This 2011 edition published by Fall River Press.

All rights reserved. No part of this publication may be reproduced, stored
in a retrieval system, or transmitted, in any form or by any means, electronic,
mechanical, photocopying, recording, or otherwise, without prior written
permission from the publisher.

Cover design by Chika Azuma
Cover photograph © Susan Trigg

ISBN 978-1-4351-2959-7

Manufactured in the United States of America

2 4 6 8 10 9 7 5 3

www.sterlingpublishing.com

Contents

REVERENTIAL LOVE

ADORING LOVE

MARRIED LOVE

LOVING COUPLES

FOR ANN

Introduction

"Heaven is unchangeable. Who can say so of love and letters?" When Henrietta Howard, Countess of Suffolk, made this observation in a letter to Lord Peterborough early in the eighteenth century, she could scarcely have known that the enamored lord's love letters, and her responses to them, would centuries hence be a significant part of the legacy by which she is remembered. She's not alone in that regard. Many famous men and women of the past are remembered today almost exclusively for the love letters they wrote, or that were written to them.

If love letters are not as old as love itself, then they are certainly as old as the art of letter writing. They comprise a literary subgenre more than a thousand years old, and they represent the work not only of esteemed men and women of arts and letters, but also of royals, statesmen, clergy, soldiers, politicians, scientists, philosophers, and others.

The World's Greatest Love Letters celebrates the love letter as a literary form, and love itself as an emotion that draws out from the lovestruck humor, pathos, poignance, charm, wit, and other attributes that distinguish and define our humanity. The letters I have selected for inclusion here represent, to my mind, many of the greatest expressions of love ever committed to paper. Their eloquence and passion are undeniable, and often quite surprising, considering their sources. We would expect memorable love letters from Lord Byron, Percy Shelley, John Keats, and other poets who regularly grappled with strong feelings in their verse, but who would have thought Napoleon Bonaparte to be such a passionate romantic, who regularly dashed off torrid mash notes to his beloved wife Josephine in the midst of his many battle campaigns. Henry VIII, who engineered the executions of two of his six wives, is usually regarded as one of history's most heartless tyrants, yet the letters in which he courts one of those unfortunates, Anne Boleyn, reveal a monarch chastened by love and subservient to the affections of his intended. Poet Alexander

Pope seemed to be incapable of writing anything that did not reflect the cool reason of the Age of Enlightenment that his writings epitomized, so how startling to read his missive to Lady Mary Wortley Montagu in which he expresses "a burning desire to see your soul stark naked."

I have grouped the letters selected into twelve very subjectively defined sections, determined solely by how we, viewing them from a modern perspective, might categorize their outpourings of sentiment. "Refined Love" features letters whose writers are as much concerned with discussing love in the abstract as making love to their recipients. There are letters of platonic love, and in the case of Mary Wollstonecraft's letter to Captain Gilbert Imlay, an early letter in an exchange that would grow more passionate over time. Some of the most heartfelt but saddest letters are grouped in the category "Unrequited Love," whose writers pine for lovers that they know will never love them as they do, or even reciprocate affection. At least one of these exchanges had a happy ending: Victor Hugo courted Adèle Foucher through letters until his disapproving mother died, after which he married her. "Playful Love" features some of the most whimsically romantic letters ever written, while "Reverential Love" shows how, for some romantics, love was tantamount to religious experience, and even inseparable from their religious beliefs. The category entitled "Adoring Love" speaks for itself: the letters gathered here are outspoken in their declarations of love, and the volatile passions they express are hampered only by the limitations of their syntax. The letters in "Married Love" capture couples whose love was consummated, or intended to culminate, in matrimony. It includes Sir Walter Raleigh's heartrending letter to his wife, in which he extols his love for her and their children with his execution imminent. Also included is Lord Nelson's wistful expression of marriage in the future to Lady Emma Hamilton, a union that did not occur before Nelson was killed at the Battle of Trafalgar in the Napoleonic Wars.

In a few rare instances, letter writers and their recipients were equally articulate in their exchanges. These letters are grouped in call-

and-response fashion in the category "Loving Couples." Included here are several exchanges between Lord Peterborough and Henrietta Howard, outtakes from one of the wittiest exchanges of amorous repartee on record, and letters exchanged between Robert Browning and Elizabeth Barrett, whose courtship in letters would fill an entire volume. The letters exchanged by Henry Frederick, Duke of Cumberland and his lover Lady Grosvenor are especially interesting, if only because they became evidence in a suit brought against the duke for "criminal conversation" (i.e., adultery) with his lover. The letters in "Long-Distance Love" are full of the tortured emotions of lovers separated geographically from one another by their duties and responsibilities. Some are written by military leaders from the battlefield; many of their despondent writers are unaware that they have just missed a letter posted by their lover. "Mad Love" is often hard to distinguish from "Bad Love," but in both of these categories letter writers voice feelings that incline toward the morbid and self-destructive. Affairs often end badly for one or both lovers, and letters capturing their regrets appear in "Love on the Rocks."

In "The World's Greatest Lover," I group a selection of letters by the writer whose love letters I feel distinguish him as the most sincerely romantic writer of all time. Spoiler alert: it's the poet John Keats, whose love for Fanny Brawne was reciprocated, but never consummated. When the young Keats met Fanny, he was dying of tuberculosis and the imminence of death doubtless contributed to his letters' honesty of feeling and lack of pretense. Keats moved to Italy shortly before his death, and found himself incapable of writing to Fanny in the ensuing months. His last letter to a friend, asking for a report back on her and her welfare, is emotionally devastating.

Fanny's letters to Keats do not exist, because Keats asked that they be destroyed after his death. His wish is a reminder to us that the letters we read in this volume were private, and never intended to be shared with any others but their recipients. As such, their writers — even those who published regularly—often threw off the yoke of dignified reserve, to express their feelings with uncommon candor and intensity. These letters offer a secret glimpse into the thoughts and feelings of those emboldened to put into words that most delicate and mystifying of all sentiments—love.

—MICHAEL KELAHAN
New York, 2011

REFINED
LOVE

Alexander Pope to Lady Mary Wortley Montagu
(1716)

The more I examine my own mind, the more romantic I find myself. Methinks it is a noble spirit of contradiction to fate and fortune, not to give up those that are snatched from us, but to follow them with warmer zeal, the further they are removed from the sense of it.

Sure flattery never travelled so far as three thousand miles; it is now only for truth, which overtakes all things, to reach you at this distance. It is a generous piece of popery that pursues even those who are to be eternally absent, into another world; let it be right or wrong, the very extravagance is a sort of piety.

I cannot be satisfied with strewing flowers over you, and barely honouring you as a thing lost; but must consider you as a glorious though remote being, and be sending messages and prayers after you. You have carried away so much of my esteem that what remains of it is daily languishing and dying over my acquaintance here; and, I believe, in three or four months more, I shall think Aurat-bassar as good a place as Covent Garden....

I write this in some anger; for, having frequented those people most, since you went, who seemed most in your favour. I heard nothing that concerned you talked of so often as that you went away in a black full-bottom, which I did but assert to be a bob, and was answered—love is blind. I am persuaded your wig had never suffered the criticism, but on the score of your head, and the two fine eyes that are in it.

For God's sake, madam, when you write to me, talk of yourself; there is nothing I so much desire to hear of; talk a great deal of yourself, that she who I always thought talked best may speak upon the best subject.

The shrines and reliques you tell me of no way engage my curiosity; I had ten times rather go on pilgrimage to see your face, than St. John Baptist's head.

... I doubt not but I shall be told when I come to follow you through those countries, in how pretty a manner you accommodated yourself to the customs of the true believers.... But if my fate be such, that this body of mine (which is as ill-matched to my mind, as any wife to her husband) be left behind in the journey, let the epitaph of Tibullus be set over it:—

> Here, stopped by hasty death, Alexis lies,
> Who crossed half Europe, led by Wortley's eyes.

I shall at least be sure to meet you in the next world, if there be any truth in our new doctrine of the day of judgment. Since your body is so full of fire, and capable of such solar notions as your letter describes, your soul can never be long going to the fixed stars, where I intend to settle; or else you may find me in the milky way; because Fontenelle assures us, the stars are so crowded there, that a man may stand upon one and talk to his friend on another. From thence, with a good telescope, what do you think one should take such a place as this world for? I fancy, for the devil's rookery, where the inhabitants are ready to deafen and destroy one another with eternal noise and hunger. ... I can only add my desire of being always thought yours, and of being told I am thought so by yourself whenever you would make me as happy as I can be at this distance.

Samuel Johnson to Mrs. Thrale
(1777)

Dearest Madam,

You talk of writing and writing, as if you had all the writing to yourself. If our correspondence were printed, I am sure posterity—for posterity is always the author's favourite—would say that I am a good writer too. To sit down so often with nothing to say,—to say something so often, almost without consciousness of saying and without any remembrance of having said,—is a power of which I will not violate my modesty by boasting; but I do not believe everybody has it.

Some, when they write to their friends, are all affection, some wise and sententious, some strain their powers for efforts of gaiety, some write news, and some write secrets; but to make a letter without affection, without wisdom, without gaiety, without news, and without a secret, is, doubtless, the great epistolic art.

In a man's letters, you know, madam, his soul lies naked. His letters are only the mirror of his heart. Whatever passes within him is there shown undisguised in its natural progress; nothing is invented, nothing distorted; you see systems in their elements, you discover actions in their motives.

Of this great truth, sounded by the knowing to the ignorant, and so echoed by the ignorant to the knowing, what evidence have you now before you? Is not my soul laid open before you in these veracious pages? Do you not see me reduced to my first principles? This is the pleasure of corresponding with a friend, where doubt and distrust have no place, and everything is said as it is thought. These are the letters by which souls are united, and by which minds naturally in unison move each other as they are moved themselves. I know, dearest lady, that in the perusal of this—such is the consanguinity of our intellects—you will be touched as I am touched. I have indeed concealed nothing from you, nor do I ever expect to repent of having thus opened my heart. I am, &c.,

SAMUEL JOHNSON

Robert Burns to Ellison Begbie
(1780)

I have often thought it a peculiarly unlucky circumstance in love, that though in every other situation in life telling the truth is not only the safest, but actually by far the easiest way of proceeding, a lover is never under greater difficulty in acting, nor never more puzzled for expression than when his passion is sincere and his intentions are honourable.

I do not think that it is very difficult for a person of ordinary capacity to talk of love and fondness which are not felt, and to make vows of constancy and fidelity which are never intended to be performed, if he be villain enough to practise such detestable conduct; but to a man whose heart glows with the principles of integrity and truth, and who sincerely loves a woman of amiable person, uncommon refinement of sentiment, and purity of manners, to such a one in such circumstances, I can assure you my dear, from my own feelings at this present moment, courtship is a task indeed. There is such a number of foreboding fears and distrustful anxieties crowd into my mind when I am in your company, or when I sit down to write to you, that what to speak or what to write I am altogether at a loss.

There is one rule which I have hitherto practised and which I shall invariably keep with you and that is, honestly to tell you the plain truth. There is something so mean and unmanly in the acts of dissimulation and falsehood that I am surprised they can be acted by any one in so noble, so generous a passion as virtuous love. No, my dear E., I shall never endeavour to gain your favour by such detestable practices. If you will be so good and so generous as to admit me for your partner, your companion, your bosom friend through life, there is nothing on this side of eternity shall give me greater transport: but I shall never think of purchasing your hand by any arts unworthy of a man, and, I will add, of a Christian.

There is one thing my dear, which I earnestly request of you and it is this that you should soon either put an end to my hopes by a peremptory refusal or cure me of my fears by a generous consent.

It would oblige me much if you would send me a line or two when convenient. I shall only add further that if a behaviour regulated (though perhaps but very imperfectly) by the rules of honour, and virtue of a heart devoted to love and esteem you, and an earnest endeavour to promote your happiness—if these are qualities you would wish in a friend, in a husband, I hope you shall ever find them in your real friend and sincere lover,

R. B.

Horace Walpole to the Two Misses Berry
(1789)

I have received at once most kind letters from you both, too kind, for you both talk of gratitude. Mercy on me ! which is the obliged, and which is the gainer? Two charming beings, whom everybody likes and approves, and who yet can be pleased with the company and conversation and old stories of a Methusalem? or I, who at the end of my days have fallen into more agreeable society than ever I knew at any period of my life? I will say nothing of your persons, sense, or accomplishments, but where, united with all those, could I find so much simplicity, void of pretensions and affectation? This from any other man would sound like compliment and flattery; but in me, who have appointed myself your guardian, it is a duty to tell you of your merits, that you may preserve and persevere in them. If ever I descry any faults, I will tell you as freely of them. Be just what you are, and you may dare my reproofs.

I will restrain even reproaches, tho' in jest, if it puts my sweet Agnes to the trouble of writing when she does not care for it. It is the extreme quality of my affection for both that makes me jealous if I do not receive equal tokens of friendship from both; and though nothing is more just than the observation of two sisters repeating the same ideas, yet never was that remark so ill applied. Tho' your minds are so congenial, I have long observed how originally each of you expresses her thoughts. I could repeat to you expressions of both, which I remember as distinctly as if I had only known either of you.

For the future there shall be perfect liberty among us. Either of you shall write when she pleases; while my letters are inseparably meant to both, tho' the direction may contain but one name, lest the postman should not comprehend a double address....

Mary Wollstonecraft to Captain Gilbert Imlay (1793)

I obey an emotion of my heart which made me think of wishing thee, my love, good-night, before I go to rest, with more tenderness than I can tomorrow when writing a hasty line or two under Colonel ——'s eye. You can scarcely imagine with what pleasure I anticipate the day when we are to begin almost to live together; and you would smile to hear how many plans of employment I have in my head now that I am confident my heart has found peace in your bosom. Cherish me with that dignified tenderness which I have only found in you, and your own dear girl will try to keep under a quickness of feeling that has sometimes given you pain. Yes, I will be *good*, that I may deserve to be happy, and whilst you love me, I cannot again fall into that miserable state which renders life a burden almost too heavy to be borne.

But good-night. *God bless you.* Sterne says that is equal to a kiss; yet I would rather give you the kiss into the bargain, glowing with gratitude to Heaven and affection to you. I like the word *affection* because it signifies something habitual, and we are soon to meet to try whether we have mind enough to keep our hearts warm.

Yours,

MARY WOLLSTONECRAFT

Maria Branwell to Patrick Brontë
(1812)

With the sincerest pleasure do I retire from company to converse with him whom I love beyond all others. Could my beloved friend see my heart he would then be convinced that the affection I bear him is not at all inferior to that which he feels for me—indeed I sometimes think that in truth and constancy it excels. But do not think from this that I entertain any suspicions of your sincerity—no, I firmly believe you to be sincere and generous, and doubt not in the least that you feel all you express. In return, I entreat that you will do me the justice to believe that you have not only a *very large portion* of my *affection* and *esteem*, but *all* that I am capable of feeling, and from henceforth measure my feelings by your own. Unless my love for you were very great how could I so contentedly give up my home and all my friends—a home I loved so much that I have often thought nothing could bribe me to renounce it for any great length of time together, and friends with whom I have been so long accustomed to share all the vicissitudes of joy and sorrow? Yet these have lost their weight, and though I cannot always think of them without a sigh, yet the anticipation of sharing with you all the pleasures and pains, the cares and anxieties of life, of contributing to your comfort and becoming the companion of your pilgrimage, is more delightful to me than any other prospect which this world can possibly present.

Elizabeth B. Barrett to Robert Browning
(1846)

I was thinking the other day that certainly and after all (or rather before all) I had loved you all my life unawares, that is, the idea of you. Women begin for the most part, (if ever so very little given to reverie) by meaning, in an aside to themselves, to love such and such an ideal, seen sometimes in a dream and sometimes in a book, and forswearing their ancient faith as the years creep on. I say a book, because I remember a friend of mine who looked everywhere for the original of Mr. Ward's "Tremaine," because nothing would do for *her*, she insisted, except just *that* excess of so-called refinement, with the book-knowledge and the conventional manners, (*loue qui peut*, Tremaine), and ended by marrying a lieutenant in the Navy who could not spell. Such things happen every day, and cannot be otherwise, say the wise:—and *this* being otherwise with *me* is miraculous compensation for the trials of many years, though such abundant, overabundant compensation, that I cannot help fearing it is too much, as I know that you are too good and too high for me, and that by the degree in which I am raised up you are let down, for us two to find a level to meet on. One's ideal must be above one, as a matter of course, you know. It is as far as one can reach with one's eyes (soul-eyes), not reach to touch. And here is mine . . . shall I tell you? . . . even to the visible outward sign of the black hair and the complexion (why you might ask my sisters!) yet I would not tell you, if I could not tell you afterwards that, if it had been red hair quite, it had been the same thing, only I prove the coincidence out fully and make you smile half.

Yet indeed I did not fancy that I was to love you when you came to see me—no indeed . . . any more than I did your caring on your side. My ambition when we began our correspondence, was simply that you should forget I was a woman (being weary and *blasée* of the empty written gallantries, of which I have had my share and all the more perhaps from my peculiar position which made them so without consequence), that you should forget *that* and let us be friends, and consent to teach me what you knew better than I, in art and human nature, and give me your sympathy in the meanwhile. I am a great hero-worshipper and had admired your poetry for years, and to feel that you liked to write to me and be written to was a pleasure and a pride, as I used to tell you I am sure, and then your letters were not like other letters, as I must not tell you again. Also you *influenced* me, in a way in which no one else did. For instance, by two or three half words you made me see you, and other people had delivered orations on the same subject quite without effect. I surprised everybody in this house by consenting to see you. Then, when you came, you never went away. I mean I had a sense of your presence constantly. Yes . . . and to prove how free that feeling was from the remotest presentiment of what has occurred, I said to Papa in my unconsciousness the next morning . . . "it is most extraordinary how the idea of Mr. Browning does beset me—I suppose it is not being used to see strangers, in some degree—but it haunts me . . . it is a persecution." On which he smiled and said that "it was not grateful to my friend to use such a word." When the letter came . . .

Do you know that all that time I was frightened of you? frightened in this way. I felt as if you had a power over me and meant to use it, and that I could not breathe or speak very differently from what you chose to make me. As to my thoughts, I had it in my head somehow that you read *them* as you read the newspaper—examined them, and fastened them down writhing under your long entomological pins—ah, do you remember the entomology of it all?

But the power was used upon *me*—and I never doubted that you had mistaken your own mind, the strongest of us having some exceptional weakness. Turning the wonder round in all lights, I came to what you admitted yesterday . . . yes, I saw *that* very early . . that you had come here with the intention of trying to love whomever you should find, . . . and also that what I had said about exaggerating the amount of what I could be to you, had just operated in making you more determined to justify your own presentiment in the face of mine. Well—and if that last clause was true a little, too . . . why should I be sorry now . . . and why should you have fancied for a moment, that the first could make me sorry. At first and when I did not believe that you really loved me, when I thought you deceived yourself, *then*, it was different. But now . . . now . . . when I see and believe your attachment for me, do you think that any cause in the world (except what diminished it) could render it less a source of joy to me? I mean as far as I myself am considered. Now if you ever fancy that I am *vain* of your love for me, you will be unjust, remember. If it were less dear, and less above me, I might be vain perhaps. But I may say *before* God and you, that of all the events of my life, inclusive of its afflictions, nothing has humbled me so much as your love. Right or wrong it may be, but true it *is*, and I tell you. Your love has been to me like God's own love, which makes the receivers of it kneelers.

UNREQUITED LOVE

Mary Queen of Scots to the Earl of Bothwell
(ca. 1567?)

My Lord,

If the displeasure of your absence, of your forgetfulness, the fear of danger promised by every one to your so loved person, may give me consolation, I leave it to you to judge, seeing the mishap that my cruel lot and continual misadventure has hitherto promised me, following the misfortunes and fears, as well of late, as of a long time by past, the which you do know. But for all that I will nowise accuse you, neither of your little remembrance, neither of your little care, and least of all of your promise broken, or of the coldness of your writing, since I am else so far made yours that that which pleases you is acceptable to me; and my thoughts are so willingly subdued unto yours that I suppose that all that cometh of you proceeds not of any the causes aforesaid, but rather of such as be just and reasonable, and such as I desire myself, which is the final order that you promised to take for the surety and honourable service of the only supporter of my life. For which alone I will preserve the same, and without the which I desire nought but sudden death. And to testify unto you how lowly I submit myself to your commandments I have sent you of homage by Pareis an ornament of the head, which is the chief guide of the other members. Inferring thereby that by the seizing of you in the possession of the spoil of which that is the principal, the remnant cannot be but subject unto you, and with consenting of the heart.

In place whereof, since I have else left it unto you, I send unto you one sculpture of hard stone coloured with black, engraved with tears and bones. The stone I compare to my heart, that as it is covered in one sure sepulture or harbour of your commandments, and, above all, of your name and memory, that are therein enclosed as is my heart in this ring, never to come forth while death grant unto you to one trophy of victory to my bones, as the ring is filled, in sign you have made one full conquest of me, of my heart, and in that my bones are left unto you in remembrance of your victory and my acceptable love and willingness, for to be better bestowed than I merit. The annealing that is about is black, which signifies the steadfastness of her that sends the same. The tears are without number, so are the fears to displease you, the tears for your absence, the disdain that I cannot be in outward effect yours, as I am without faintness of heart and spirit, and of good reason, though my merits were much greater than that of the most profit that ever was, and such as I desire to be, and shall take pains in conditions to imitate, for to be bestowed worthily under your governance. My only wealth receive, therefore, in as good part and the same, as I have received of your marriage in extreme joy, that which shall not part forth of my bosom till that marriage of our bodies be made in public, as a sign of all that I either hope or desire of bliss in this world.

Yet, my heart, fearing to displease you, as much in the reading hereof, as it delights me in the writing, I will make an end, after I have kissed your hand with as great affection as I pray God (oh, the only supporter of my life!) to give you long and blessed life, and to me your good favour, as the only good that I desire, and to the which I pretend. I have shown unto the bearer of this that which I have learned, knowing the credit that you give him; as she also doth, that will be forever unto you an humble and obedient lawful wife that forever dedicates unto you her heart, her body, without any change unto him I have made the possessor of my heart, of which you may hold you assured, that unto death shall no ways be changed, for evil nor good shall never make me go from it.

Henry of Navarre to Henrietta D'Entragues
(1608)

You are mistaken in your letter, for you say that I am your dear heart, and that you are not mine. I have taken away nought from you, but you have taken from me all that you could. That is one reason why there is no answer. Let not your spirit be alarmed in searching for one, for it is better to be silent when you have nothing to say that counts.

As for me, I love you so dearly that all priceless things are mere dross to me; I swear this to you, my dearest love. But do not think to nourish me on a stone after having given me bread. Be mindful of my age, my rank, my mind, and my affection, and you will do what you have not done. Good day, my all, and a million kisses.

Marianna L'Alcaforada to Noel Bouton de Chamilly
(ca. 1670?)

Will you, then, be always cold and listless! Can nothing have power to interrupt your repose! What must be done to disturb it? Must I, in your presence, throw myself into the arms of a rival? For, except this last act of inconstancy, which my love will never allow me to commit, I have given you reason to apprehend every other.

I accepted the arm of the Duke d'Almeida on the promenade; I contrived to sit near him at supper, and even whispered in his ear some trifles, which you might have taken for subjects of importance; yet I could cause no change in your countenance. Ingrate! Have you really the inhumanity to feel so little love for her who so well loves you? Have not my cares, my favors, and my truth, been worth one moment of your jealousy? Does he, who is more dear to me than peace or fame, so little value me, that he regards my loss without dismay! Alas! I tremble at the bare idea of losing you! You cast not a look upon another woman that does not cause me a dreadful shuddering; you offer not a civility upon the most trifling occasion that does not cost me twenty-four hours of despair! Yet can you see me converse under your eyes a whole evening with another, without betraying the least disquietude! Ah! you have never loved me; for too well I know what it is to love, to think that sentiments so different from mine should bear the name of love.

Lady Mary Pierrepont to Edward Wortley Montagu (ca. 1710?)

I thought to have returned no answer to your letter, but I find I am not so wise as I thought myself. I cannot forbear fixing my mind a little on that expression, though perhaps the only insincere one in your letter—"I would die to be secure of your heart, though but for a moment." Were this but true, what is there I would not do to secure you?

I will state the case to you as plainly as I can; and then ask yourself if you use me well. I have showed in every action of my life an esteem for you that at least challenges a grateful regard. I have trusted my reputation in your hands; I have made no scruple of giving you, under my own hand, an assurance of my friendship. After all this, I exact nothing from you. If you find it inconvenient for your affairs to take so small a fortune, I desire you to sacrifice nothing to me. I pretend no tie upon your honour; but in recompense for so clear and so disinterested a proceeding, must I ever receive injuries and ill-usage?

I have not the usual pride of my sex. I can bear being told I am in the wrong, but I must be told gently. Perhaps I have been indiscreet: I came young into the hurry of the world; a great innocence and an undesigning gayety may possibly have been construed coquetry and a desire of being followed, though never meant by me. I cannot answer for the observations that may be made on me. All who are malicious attack the careless and defenceless. I own myself to be both. I know not anything I can say more to show my perfect desire of pleasing you and making you easy, than to proffer to be confined with you in what manner you please. Would any woman but me renounce all the world for one? or would any man but you be insensible of such a proof of sincerity?

M.P.

Alexander Pope to Teresa Blount
(1716)

Madam,

I have so much esteem for you, and so much of the other thing, that, were I a handsome fellow, I should do you a vast deal of good: but as it is, all I am good for, is to write a civil letter, or to make a fine speech. The truth is, that considering how often and how openly I have declared love to you, I am astonished (and a little affronted) that you have not forbid my correspondence, and directly said, *See my face no more!*

It is not enough, madam, for your reputation, that you have your hands pure from the stain of such ink as might be shed to gratify a male correspondent. Alas! while your heart consents to encourage him in this lewd liberty of writing, you are not (indeed you are not) what you would so fain have me think you—a prude! I am vain enough to conclude that (like most young fellows) a fine lady's silence is consent, and so I write on—

But, in order to be as innocent as possible in this epistle, I will tell you news. You have asked me news a thousand times, at the first word you spoke to me; which some would interpret as if you expected nothing from my lips: and truly it is not a sign two lovers are together, when they can be so impertinent as to inquire what the world does. All I mean by this is, that either you or I cannot be in love with the other: I leave you to guess which of the two is that stupid and insensible creature, so blind to the other's excellences and charms.

Lord Peterborough to Henrietta Howard
(ca. 1722?)

As I can as well live without meat or sleep as without thinking of her who has possession of my soul, so, to find some relief in never having any conversation with this adored lady, I have been forced, when alone, to make many a dialogue between her and myself; but, alas! Madam, the conclusions are all in her favour, and I am often more cruelly condemned by myself,—nay, more, her indifference and almost all her rigour are approved.

Permit me to give you an account of my last duet with my partner; and as by the original articles of our scribbling treaty, you were sincerely to tell me your opinion, so remember your long silence, and give me an answer to this.

On my part I was representing to her the violence, the sincerity of my passion; but what I most insisted on was, that in most circumstances it was different from that of other men. It is true I confessed, with common lovers, she was the person I wished should grant, but with this addition, that she was the only woman that I could allow to refuse. In a word, I am resolved, nay, content, to be only hers, though it may be impossible she should ever be mine.

To bear injuries or miseries insensibly were a vain pretence; not to resent, not to feel, is impossible; but when I dare venture to think she is unjust or cruel, my revenge falls upon all of the sex but herself. I hate, detest, and renounce all other creatures in hoop petticoats, and, by a strange weakness, can only wish well to her who has the power and will to make me miserable.

Commonly lovers are animated by the gay look, the blooming cheeks, and the red lips of the mistress; but, heavens! what do I feel when I see anguish and paleness invade that charming face? My soul is in a mutiny against those powers that suffer it, and my heart perfectly melts away in tenderness. But for whom have I such concern? For that dear lady who scarce thinks of me, or scarce regretteth she makes me wretched.

But alas! it was in this last dialogue I found my misery complete; for you must know, the lady had listened with some attention. Mercy was in her looks, softness in her words, and gentleness in all her air. "Were this all true," she asked, "what could you expect?—what do you think your due?"

Never was poor mortal so dismayed. Though she was absent I had not the courage to make one imaginary request; had she been present I could only have expressed my wishes by one trembling look. Oh, wretched prodigality, where one gives all and dare demand no return! Oh, unfortunate avarice, which covets all and can merit nothing! Oh, cruel ambition, which can be satisfied with nothing less but what no man can deserve!

It was long before I could recover from the terror and amaze into which I had thrown myself. At last I ventured to make this answer: "If what I may pretend to be less than love, surely it is something more than friendship."

Samuel Johnson to Mrs. Thrale
(1782)

Since you have written to me with the attention and tenderness of ancient times, your letters give me a great part of the pleasure which a life of solitude admits. You will never bestow any share of your good-will on one who deserves better. *Those who have loved longest love best.* A sudden blaze of affection may by a single blast of coldness be extinguished; but that fondness which length of time has connected with many circumstances and occasions, though it may for a while be depressed by disgust or resentment, with or without a cause, is hourly revived by accidental recollection. To those that have been much together, everything heard and everything seen recalls some pleasure communicated, or some benefit conferred, some petty quarrel or some slight endearment. Esteem of great powers, or amiable qualities newly discovered, may embroider a day or a week, but a friendship of twenty years is interwoven with the texture of life. A friend may be often found and lost, but an *old friend* never can be found, and nature has provided that he cannot *easily* be lost.

George IV to Margaritta Fitzherbert
(ca. 1794?)

Do you indeed wish for my friendship? Ah, Margaritta, I know not how to believe you, while thus cold, thus insensible to all my desires. A meeting again refused! Who are these very good people, whom I have so much reason to dislike? They have no paternal authority over you,

I understand; why then regard their narrow prejudices? May I entreat your history? Yet I almost dread to hear an account of a life in which I am already so much interested, and which may make me still more enamoured of the dear, preverse historian. Politics I should never have mentioned to a lady, but as you seem to blame my conduct, I wish to exculpate myself in your opinion; but you must allow me to do it personally, for the subject is too long for a letter. On horseback you might permit me the pleasure of attending you. I have seen you riding with only a servant; let me join you without any. I never ride but with one here, and he shall be forbid, because my livery would carry a mark that you would not like. Your servant would not know me, and report would have nothing to say about it. I entreat you to allow me this, and to appoint an early day.

Your letters I keep as an invaluable treasure, and shall hardly be so careless of them as you expect. So young, so lovely, and yet so coldly prudent! Ah, Margaritta, would that you partook of the warmth that burns in the heart of your faithful

WALES

Mary Wollstonecraft to Captain Gilbert Imlay (1794)

I received both your letters to-day. I had reckoned on hearing from you yesterday, therefore was disappointed, though I imputed your silence to the right cause. I intended answering your kind letter immediately, that you might have felt the pleasure it gave me; but —— came in, and some other things interrupted me, so that the fine vapour has evaporated, yet leaving a sweet scent behind. I have only to tell you, what is sufficiently obvious, that the earnest desire I have shown to keep my place, or gain more ground in your heart, is a sure proof how necessary your affection is to my happiness. Still I do not think it false delicacy or foolish pride to wish that your attention to my happiness should arise *as much* from love, which is always rather a selfish passion, as reason,—that is, I want you to promote my felicity by seeking your own. For, whatever pleasure it may give me to discover your generosity of soul, I would not be dependent for your affection on the very quality I most admire. No: there are qualities in your heart which demand my affection; but unless the attachment appears to me clearly mutual, I shall labour only to esteem your character instead of cherishing a tenderness for your person.

Claire Clairmont to Lord Byron
(1815)

You bid me write short to you, and I have much to say. You also bade me believe that it was a fancy which made me cherish an attachment for you. It cannot be a fancy since you have been for the last year the object upon which every solitary moment led me to muse.

I do not expect you to love me; I am not worthy of your love. I feel you are superior, yet much to my surprise, more to my happiness, you betrayed passions I had believed no longer alive in your bosom. Shall I also have to ruefully experience the want of happiness? Shall I reject it when it is offered? I may appear to you imprudent, vicious, my opinions detestable, my theory depraved; but one thing, at least, time shall show you that I love gently and with affection, that I am incapable of anything approaching to the feeling of revenge or malice; I do assure you, your future will shall be mine, and everything you shall do or say, I shall not question.

Victor Hugo to Adèle Foucher
(1821)

This letter is quite important, Adèle. The impression it makes on you will determine our future. If I can only think calmly, and give you my ideas sanely, I shall have no difficulty in fighting against sleep to-night. I wish I could repeat to you, face to face, this serious and intimate talk I have prepared, for then I could get your answer at once,—I shall await it with the utmost impatience,—and I should be able to tell from your expression the effect of my words—the effect that is to settle the question of our happiness.

Until now, Adèle, there seems to have been one word which we have shrunk from pronouncing—the word *love*. Yet the feeling I have for you is surely love. And so it is of importance for us to know whether the sentiment which you feel is the same.

Listen! Each of us has in our bodies, in exile as it were, a spiritual something which never dies. This something, which is the essence of what is truest and purest in humanity, is the soul. The soul is the source of ecstasy and affection. Upon it depend our conceptions of God and heaven. I am writing of things which are beyond our knowledge, simply because it is necessary to do so in order that you may understand me; but as you may think that what I am saying is unusual, let me try to describe these things in simple, but reverent language.

Since the soul is superior to the body, to which it is united, it would remain on earth in painful loneliness were it not for the fact that among other human souls it may choose a companion—a partner in the trials of life and in the joys of the hereafter. When two souls, which have sought each other amid the crowd, find they have met, realize that they belong to each other, and comprehend this affinity, then it is that a union has been brought about, as pure and aspiring as themselves—a union which begun on earth will be consummated in heaven.

This union is love—genuine, complete love, such as few men can imagine. It is a love which is a religion, since the object of love is regarded as a divinity, with all the devotion and affection which turn the greatest sacrifices into the sublimest joys. Such a love you inspire in me, and such a love you will some day feel for me, although to my sorrow you do not feel it now. Your soul is capable of an angelic love. It may be, therefore, that only an angel can inspire such a love. When I think of this, I tremble.

Such a love, Adèle, is not easily understood by the world. It is appreciated only by those who are elected to great gladness or great suffering—you, for your joy, I, for my suffering. In the eyes of the world love is either a physical longing or delusion, which possession as well as absence destroys. And so people say, with a strange abuse of words, that love does not last. Love means suffering you think, Adèle? Do you seriously believe there is any suffering in ordinary love, which seems so violent and which, in realization, is so weak? No, spiritual love is eternal because it belongs to that part of us which cannot die. Our souls love, not our bodies.

Remember, however, that nothing should be urged to extremes. I do not say that the physical has no place in all this. Two souls could never be in happy union unless the bodies, which hold them, are also attractive to each other. A gracious God has effected this, thereby making marriage divine. And so, in youth, physical union serves to consummate the union of souls; so it is that in their turn, our souls, which are ever young, ever indestructible, preserve the union of the persons even after the bodies have wasted away, and are dissolved by death.

Do not fear, Adèle, about the duration of a passion which even God could not extinguish. Such a deep and lasting affection do I feel for you. It is an affection not based on the charms of person, but on spiritual qualities—an affection that leads to heaven or to hell, and which fills life with ecstasy or torture.

I have revealed my soul to you. I have spoken the language which I only speak to those who can understand. In your turn ask yourself if love means to you what it does for me, whether your soul has found its mate in my soul. Pay no attention to what a foolish world thinks, or to what is thought by the little minds around you; look into your heart, listen to its voice.

If the thoughts in this letter are real to you, if indeed you have the same affection for me that I have for you, then, my Adèle, I am thine for life—for eternity. If you fail to understand me and my love, if it all seems extravagant, then farewell. Death alone will be left, but death will have no terrors when all earthly hope is lost. Do not think, however, that I shall take my own life. There are the sick to heal, holy battles to fight, and suicide is the act of an egotist and a coward. What I meant is, that I shall sacrifice my life entirely for others, for only in that way will it seem endurable. These thoughts may seem gloomy as concerning her for whom my lips have always worn a smile, her who does not yet know my usual thoughts.

I tremble to think, Adèle, that you have not for me the love I offer you, and it is only such a love that can satisfy me. If you loved me thus, could you keep asking me as you do if I trust you? You do this so carelessly that it smacks of indifference. Still, you are offended at the most natural questions, and keep asking me whether I think your conduct censurable.

If you loved me, Adèle, as I love you, you would understand that there are a thousand things that may be done without wickedness, without wrong, but which nevertheless alarm the sensitive jealousy of my affection. Such love as I have described to you is exclusive. I myself wish for nothing, not even a glance from any other woman in the world, but I insist that no man should dare to claim anything from the woman who is mine. If I want her only, it is because I want her wholly and entirely. A look, a smile, a kiss from you are my greatest happiness. Could I patiently endure to see you give them to another, as well? Does this sensitiveness alarm you? If you loved me it would delight you. Why do you not feel this way toward me? Love is jealous, and is ingenious in inflicting pain on itself in proportion to its purity and intensity. I have always found it so. A long time ago, I remember, your little brother, then a mere child, chanced to sleep with you—I shuddered at the thought. Age and experience with the world have only confirmed this feeling in me. I fear it will be my undoing, for while it ought to increase your happiness it only makes you feel uncomfortable.

Speak freely. Make it plain to me whether you wish me such as I am or not. Our future depends upon it, but though mine is nothing to me, yours is everything. If you do not love me there is a sure and speedy way of releasing yourself. I shall not oppose you. There is a certain kind of absence that causes us to be forgotten by the indifferent. It is the absence which never ends.

One word more. Do not be astonished if this lengthy letter strikes you as sad and melancholy—your own was so cold. You really seem to believe that between us "passion is out of place." Adèle, I read your old letters again for some ray of consolation, but the difference between them and the new ones was so great that instead of consolation—

Goodbye.

Prosper Mérimée to "Unknown"
(1848)

What a strange world we are living in! But the most important and urgent thing I have to say to you is that I love you more every day. I earnestly wish you only had the courage to say as much to me.

PLAYFUL
LOVE

George Farquhar to "Penelope" Oldfield
(ca. 1700?)

~~~~~~~~~

I came, I saw, and was conquered; never had man more to say, yet can I say nothing; where others go to save their souls, there have I lost mine; but I hope that Divinity which has the justest title to its service has received it; but I will endeavour to suspend these raptures for a moment, and talk calmly.—

Nothing on earth, madam, can charm beyond your wit but your beauty: after this not to love you would proclaim me a fool; and to say I did when I thought otherwise would pronounce me a knave; if anybody called me either I should resent it; and if you but think me either I shall break my heart.

You have already, madam, seen enough of me to create a liking or an aversion; your sense is above your sex, then let your proceeding be so likewise, and tell me plainly what I have to hope for. Were I to consult my merits my humility would chide any shadow of hope; but after a sight of such a face whose whole composition is a smile of good nature, why should I be so unjust as to suspect you of cruelty. Let me either live in *London* and be happy or retire again to my desert to check my vanity that drew me thence; but let me beg to receive my sentence from your own mouth, that I may hear you speak and see you look at the same time; then let me be unfortunate if I can.

If you are not the lady in mourning that sat upon my right hand at church, you may go to the devil, for I'm sure you're a witch.

George Farquhar to "Penelope" Oldfield
(ca. 1700?)

Madam,

If I haven't begun thrice to write and as often thrown away my pen, may I never take it up again; my head and my heart have been at cuffs about you these two long hours,—says my head, you're a coxcomb for troubling your noddle about a lady whose beauty is as much above your pretensions as your merit is below her love.

Then answers my heart,—Good Mr. Head, you're a blockhead. I know Mr. F——r's merit better than you; as for your part, I know you to be as whimsical as the devil, and changing with every new notion that offers, but for my share I am fixt, and can stick to my opinion of a lady's merit for ever, and if the fair she can secure an interest in me, Monsieur Head, you may go whistle."

Come, come, (answered my head) you, Mr. Heart, are always leading the gentleman into some inconvenience or other; was it not you that first enticed him to talk to this lady? Your damn'd confounded warmth made him like this lady, and your busy impertinence has made him write to her; your leaping and skipping disturbs his sleep by night and his good humour by day: in short, sir, I will hear no more on't; I am head, and will be obeyed.

You lie, sir, replied my heart (being very angry), I am head in matters of love, and if you don't give your consent, you shall be forced, for I am sure that in this case all the members will be on my side. What say you, gentlemen Hands!

Oh (say the hands), we would not forego the tickling pleasure of touching a delicious white soft skin for the world.

Well, what say you, Mr. Tongue?

Zounds, says the linguist, there is more extasy in speaking three soft words of Mr. Heart's suggesting than whole orations of Signior Head's, so I am for the lady, and here's honest neighbour, Lips, will stick to't."

By the sweet power of kisses, that we will, (replied the lips) and presently some other worthy members, standing up for the Heart, they laid violent hands *(nemine contradicente)* on poor Head, and knocked out his brains. So now, madam, behold me as perfect a lover as any in Christendom, my heart firmly dictating every word I say. The little rebel throws itself into your power, and if you don't support it in the cause it has taken up for your sake, think what will be the condition of the headless and heartless

FARQUHAR

Richard Steele to Mary Scurlock
(1707)

Madam,

It is the hardest thing in the world to be in love, and yet attend to business. As for me all who speak to me find me out, and I must lock myself up, or other people will do it for me.

A gentleman asked me this morning, "What news from Lisbon?" and I answered, "She is exquisitely handsome." Another desired to know when I had been last at Hampton Court. I replied, "It will be on Tuesday come se'nnight." Pr'ythee, allow me at least to kiss your hand before that day, that my mind may be in some composure. O love!

> A thousand torments dwell about thee,
> Yet who would live to live without thee?

Methinks I could write a volume to you; but all the language on earth would fail in saying how much and with what disinterested passion,

I am ever yours,

RICH. STEELE

Jonathan Swift to "Stella" (Esther Johnson) (1710)

So here is Mistress Stella again with her two eggs, &c. My Shower admired with you ; why the Bishop of Clogher says he has seen something of mine of the same sort, better than the Shower. I suppose he means the Morning; but it is not half so good. I want your judgment of things and not your country's. How does M. D. like it? and do they taste it *all*, &c? I will break your head in good earnest, young woman, for your nasty jest about Mrs. Barton. Unlucky sluttikin, what a word is there? Faith I was thinking yesterday when I was with her whether she could break them or no, and it quite spoiled my imagination. Mrs. Wall, does Stella win as she pretends? No indeed, doctor, she loses always, and will play so venturesomely, how can she win? See here now, are not you an impudent, lying slut?

Pshaw! I must be writing to those dear saucy brats every night, whether I will or no, let me have what business I will, or come home ever so late, or be ever so sleepy; but an old saying and a true one —

> Be you lords, or be you earls,
> You must write to naughty girls.

Henrietta Howard to Lord Peterborough
(ca. 1722?)

I cannot much wonder that men are always so liberal in making presents of their hearts, yet I cannot help admiring the women who are so very fond of these acquisitions. Let us consider the ingredients that make up the heart of man.

It is composed of dissimulation, self-love, vanity, inconstancy, equivocation, and such fine qualities. Who, then, would make that a present to a lady, when they have one of their own so very like it?

A man's heart never wants the outward appearance of truth and sincerity. Every lover's heart is so finely varnished with them that it is almost impossible to distinguish the true from the false ones. According to my observations the false ones have generally the finest gloss.

When your Lordship asks a heart for a heart, you seem to reckon them all of equal value. I fancy you think them all false ones, which is the surest way not to be often imposed upon. I beg your lordship, in this severe opinion of hearts, to except mine as well as your own.

If you were so happy as to be the owner of a false heart, you would esteem it as the most perfect present for a lady; for should you make her a present of such a one as yours was before you parted with it, it is fifty to one whether you would receive a true one in return.

Therefore, let everyone who expects an equivalent for his heart be provided with a false one, which is equally fit for the most professed lover. It will burn, flame, bleed, pant, sigh, and receive as many darts, and appear altogether as charming as a true one. Besides, it does not in the least embarrass the bearer, and I think your Lordship was always a lover of liberty.

Laurence Sterne to Lady P.
(ca. 1765?)

There is a strange mechanical effect produced in writing a billet-doux within a stone cast of the lady who engrosses the heart and soul of an *inamorato*. For this cause (but mostly because I am to dine in this neighbourhood) have I, Tristram Shandy, come forth from my lodgings to a coffee-house, the nearest I could find to my dear Lady ——'s house, and have called for a sheet of gilt paper to try the truth of this article of my creed—now for it—

O my dear Lady, what a dishclout of a soul hast thou made of me!— I think, by the by, this a little too familiar an introduction for so unfamiliar a situation as I stand in with you—where, heaven knows, I am kept at a distance and despair of getting an inch nearer you, with all the steps and windings I can think of to recommend myself to you. Would not any man in his senses run diametrically from you, and as far as his legs would carry him, rather than thus causelessly, foolishly and foolhardily, expose himself afresh and afresh, where his heart and his reason tell him he shall be sure to come off loser, if not totally undone.

Why would you tell me you would be glad to see me? Does it give you pleasure to make me more unhappy, or does it add to your triumph, that your eyes and lips have turned a man into a fool, whom the rest of the town is courting as a wit?

I am a fool, the weakest, the most ductile, the most tender fool that ever woman tried the weakness of, and the most unsettled in my purposes and resolutions of recovering my right mind.

It is but an hour ago that I kneeled down and swore I never would come near you, and after saying my Lord's Prayer for the sake of the close, *of not being led into temptation*, out I sallied like any Christian hero, ready to take the field against the world, the flesh and the devil;

not doubting but I should finally trample them all down under my feet.

And now I am got so near you, within this vile stone's cast of your house, I feel myself drawn into a vortex, that has turned my brain upside downwards; and though I had purchased a box ticket to carry me to Miss ——'s benefit, yet I knew very well that was a single line directed to me to let me know Lady —— would be alone at seven, and suffer me to spend the evening with her, she would infallibly see everything verified I have told her.

I dine at Mr C——r's in Wigmore Street, in this neighbourhood, where I shall stay till seven, in hopes you purpose to put me to this proof. If I hear nothing by that time, I shall conclude you are better disposed of, and shall take a sorry hack and sorrily jog on to the play. Curse on the word, I know nothing but sorrow, except the one thing that I love you (perhaps foolishly, but) most sincerely,

L. STERNE

Robert Burns (Sylvander) to
Mrs. Agnes McLehose (Clarinda)
(1788)

The attraction of Love, I find, is in an inverse proportion to the attraction of the Newtonian philosophy. In the system of Sir Isaac, the nearer objects are to one another the stronger is the attractive force: in my system, every milestone that marked my progress from Clarinda awakened a keener pang of attachment to her. How do you feel, my love? is your heart ill at ease? I fear it. God forbid that these persecutors should harass that peace which is more precious to me than my own! Be assured I shall ever think of you, muse on you, and, in my hours of devotion, pray for you.

The hour that you are not in all my thoughts—"be that hour darkness! let the shadows of death cover it! let it not be numbered in the hours of day!"

> When I forget my darling theme,
> Be my tongue mute! my fancy paint no more!
> And, dead to joy, forget my heart to beat!

I have just met with my old friend, the ship-captain—guess my pleasure! To meet you could alone have given me more. My brother William, too, the young saddler, has come to Glasgow to meet me; and here are we three spending the evening.

I arrived here too late to write by post; but I'll wrap half a dozen sheets of blank paper together, and send it by the Fly, under the name of a parcel. You shall hear from me next post town. I would write you a longer letter, but for the present circumstances of my friend.

Adieu, my Clarinda! I am just going to propose your health by way of grace-drink.

SYLVANDER

Horace Walpole to the Two Misses Berry
(1789)

Such unwriting wives I never knew! and a shame it is for an author, and what is more, for a printer, to have a Couple so unlettered. I can find time amidst all the hurry of my shop to write small quartos to them continually. In France, where nuptiality is not the virtue the most in request, a wife will write to her consort, tho' the doux billet should contain but two sentences, of which I will give you a precedent: A lady sent the following to her spouse: "Je vous écrit, parceque je n'ai rien à faire; et je finis, parceque je n'ai rien à vous dire." I do not wish for quite so laconic a poulet; besides, your ladyships *can* write.

Lord Nelson to Lady Emma Hamilton
(1801)

Having, my truly dearest friend, got through a great deal of business, I am enabled to do justice to my private feelings, which are fixed ever on you and about you, whenever the public service does not arrest my attention. I have read all your kind and affectionate letters, and have read them frequently over and committed them to the flames much against my inclination. There was one I rejoiced not to have read at the time. It was where you consented to dine and sing with ——. Thank God it was not so. I could not have borne it, and now less than ever, but I now know he never can dine with you, for you would go out of the house rather than suffer it. And as to letting him hear you sing, I only hope he will be struck deaf, and you dumb, sooner than such a thing should happen; but I know it now never can.

Daniel Webster to Josephine Seaton
(1844)

My dear Josephine,

I fear you got a wetting last evening, as it rained fast soon after you left our door; and I avail myself of the return of your bonnet to express the wish that you are well this morning, and without cold.

I have demanded parlance with your bonnet; have asked it how many tender looks it has noticed to be directed under it; what soft words it has heard, close to its side; in what instances an air of triumph has caused it to be tossed; and whether, ever, and when, it has quivered from trembling emotions proceeding from below. But it has proved itself a faithful keeper of secrets, and would answer none of my questions. It only remained for me to attempt to surprise it into confession, by pronouncing sundry names one after another. It seemed quite unmoved by most of these, but at the apparently unexpected mention of one, I thought its ribbands decidedly fluttered!

I gave it my parting good wishes, hoping that it might never cover an aching head, and that the eyes which it protects from the rays of the sun, may know no tears but of joy and affection.

Yours, dear Josephine, with affectionate regard,

DANIEL WEBSTER

REVERENTIAL
LOVE

Margery Brews to John Paston
(1477)

Unto my right well-beloved Valentine, John Paston, Esq.,
be this billet delivered.

Right reverend and worshipful and my right well-beloved Valentine,
I recommend me unto you, full heartily desiring to hear of your welfare,
which I beseech Almighty God long to preserve unto his pleasure and
your heart's desire. And if it please you to hear of *my* welfare, I am not in
good health of body or of heart, nor shall be till I hear from you.

> For there wots no creature what pain I endure,
> And for to be deed, I dare not it discure.

And my lady, my mother, has laboured the matter to my father full
diligently, but she can no more get than ye know of, for the which God
knoweth I am full sorry. But if that ye love me, as I trust verily that ye do,
ye will not leave me therefor; for if *ye* had not half the livelihood that ye
have, for to do the greatest labour that any woman alive might, I would
not forsake *you*.

> And if ye command me to keep true wherever I go,
> I wis I will do all my might you to love and never no mo';
> And if my friends say that I do amiss,
> They shall not prevent me so for to do.
> My heart me bids evermore to love you
> Truly over all earthly thing,
> And if they be never so wroth
> I trust it shall be better in time coming.

No more to you at this time, but the Holy Trinity have you in his keeping. And I beseech you that this billet be not seen of no earthly creature save only yourself, &c.

And this letter was indite at Topcroft with full heavy heart

By your own

Margery Brews

Richard Calle to Margery Paston
(1469)

Mine own lady and mistress, and before God very true wife, I with heart full sorrowful recommend me to you, as he that cannot be merry, nor nought shall be till it is otherwise with us than it is yet, for this life that we lead now is neither pleasure to God nor to the world, considering the great bond of matrimony that is betwixt us, and also the great love that hath been and, as I trust, is yet betwixt us, and on my part never greater. Wherefore I beseech Almighty God comfort us as soon as it pleases him, for we that ought of very right to be most together are most asunder: meseemeth it is a thousand years ago since I spake with you. I had liever than all the good in the world I might be with you. Alas, alas, good lady, full little remember they what they do that keep us asunder; four times in the year are they cursed that hinder matrimony; it causeth many men to deem they have large conscience in other matters as well as herein. But what lady suffers as ye have done? Make ye as merry as ye can, for I wis, lady, at the long way, God will of his right wiseness help his servants that mean truly and would live according to his laws.

I understand, lady, that ye have made as much sorrow for me as any gentlewoman hath had in the world. Would God all the sorrow ye have had, had rested upon me, so that ye had been discharged of it, for I wis, dear lady, it is to me a death that ye be treated otherwise than ye ought to be. This is a painful life that we lead. I cannot live thus without it be a great displeasure to God.

Also like you to wit that I sent you a letter by my lad, from London, and he told me that he might not speak with you, there was made so great await upon him and upon you both. He told me John Thresher came to him in your name, and said that ye sent him to my lad for a ring or a token which I should have sent you, but he trusted him not; he would not deliver him none. After that he brought him a ring saying that ye sent it him, commanding him that he should deliver the letter or token to him, which I conceive was not by your sending; it was by my mistress's and Sir James's advice. Alas! what mean they? I suppose they deem we be not ensured together, and if they do so I marvel, for then they are not well advised, remembering the plainness that I break to my mistress in the beginning, and I suppose *by* you both, and ye did as ye ought to do of very right; and if you have done the contrary, as I am informed ye have done, ye did neither conscientiously nor to the pleasure of God, unless ye did it for fear, and for the time to please such as were at that time about you, and if ye so did it for this service it was for a reasonable cause, considering the great and unbearable calling upon that ye had, and many an untrue tale was told you of me, which God knows I was never guilty of.

My lad told me that my mistress, your mother, asked him if he had brought any letter to you; and many other things she bear him on hand, and among all other, at the last she said to him that I would not make her acquainted with the beginning, but she supposed I would at the ending; and as to that, God knows she knew first of me and none other. I wot not what her mistressship meant; for, by my troth, there is no gentlewoman alive that my heart tendereth more than it doth her, nor is loather to displease, saving only your person, which of very right I ought to tender and love best, for I am bound thereto by the law of God, and so will do while I live, whatsoever befalls. I suppose, and ye tell them solemnly the truth, they will not damn their souls for us; though I tell them the truth, they will not believe me as well as they will do you; and therefore, good lady, at the reverence of God, be plain to them and tell them the truth, and if they will in no wise agree thereto, betwixt God, the Devil, and them be it; and that peril that we should be in, I beseech God it may lie upon them and not upon us. . . .

Madame, I am afraid to write you, for I understand ye have showed the letters that I have sent you before this time, but I pray you let no creature see this letter. As soon as ye have read it, let it be burnt, for I would no man should see it in no wise. Ye had no writing from me this two years, nor I would not send ye no more; therefore I remit all this matter to your wisdom. Almighty Jesu preserve, keep, and give you your heart's desire, which I wot well would be to God's pleasure.

This letter was written with as great pain as ever wrote I thing in my life; for in good faith I have been right sick, and yet am not very well at ease. God amend it, &c.

Margaret of Valois to James, Lord of Chanvallon (ca.1580?)

By the perfection of the work, one recognises not only the skill of the artisan, but how attentively he has applied himself to it. Nothing is more certain, that the most difficult works require a mind entirely absorbed with them and sensitive of the difference between what is mechanically, or lightly performed and what is pleasing or even absorbing to the affection.

Thus, dear heart, may one judge by the subtle and faithful description you give of the nature and sympathy of our love—the soul study, which pleases your heart, exalts it, and gives it a contempt for things low and earthly while raising it to a conception of what is highest and most beautiful, bearing testimony, as it were, to its permanency and invincibility.

Thus it occupies all its functions with that which its intelligence and taste have chosen, like those thrice happy spirits returned to receive in the bosom of the infinite some new daily joy which captivates with a ravishment so exquisite that, if the saints were in such a state and I reconciled to the Huguenots, I do not believe that they would hear our prayers. In vain others supplicate me. For them I am deaf, blind, and without feeling. My soul is occupied with a thought so beautiful, that it can never be diverted; and if I were only able to obey my inclination, whether in thought or action, I would render love so devoted and saintly, that no hermit, who had retired from the world to give himself up to adoration, could equal my ecstasy.

What is there for me in freedom, or life, if I be deprived for a single day of your divine presence, of the power to satisfy my soul with the insatiable pleasure of so beautiful a sight! I would desire no greater happiness than that expressed by that sentence of Saint Paul, in thee are my refuge and my strength—for in a joy so complete the lover is transfigured by love, and I would have you to partake of my felicity.

In you, and in you alone, my soul reposes. And thus I would have the physical imitate the spiritual in so blissful a communion. I consider my life as nought until your beautiful hand guided it.

Oliver Cromwell to His Wife, Elizabeth
(1651)

My Dearest,

I could not satisfy myself to omit this post, although I have not much to write; yet indeed I love to write to my dear, who is very much in my heart. It joys me to hear thy soul prospereth; the Lord increase his favours to thee more and more. The great good thy soul can wish is, that the Lord lift upon thee the light of his countenance, which is better than life. The Lord bless all thy good counsel and example to all those about thee, and hear all thy prayers, and accept thee always.

Friedrich Klopstock to Meta Möller
(ca. 1751?)

With what transport do I think of you, my Meta, my only treasure, my wife! When I fancy I behold you, my mind is filled with the heavenly thoughts which so often fervently and delightfully occupy it; and while I think of you, they are still more fervent, more delightful. They glow in my breast, but no words can express them. You are dearer to me than all who are connected with me by blood or by friendship, dearer than all which is dear to me besides in creation. My sister, my friend, you are mine by love, by pure and holy love, which Providence (O how grateful am I for the blessing,) has made the inhabitant of my soul upon earth. It appears to me that you were born my twin sister in Paradise. At present, indeed, we are not there, but we shall return thither. Since we have so much happiness here, what shall we have there?

Remember me to all our friends. My Meta, my forever beloved, I am entirely yours.

Robert Burns to Ellison Begbie
(1780)

I verily believe, my dear E., that the pure genuine feelings of love are as rare in the world as the pure genuine principles of virtue and piety. . . . I don't know how it is, my dear, for though except your company there is nothing on earth gives me so much pleasure as writing to you, yet it never gives me those giddy raptures so much talked of among lovers. I have often thought that if so well-grounded affection be not really a part of virtue, 'tis something extremely akin to it. Whenever the thought of my E. warms my heart every feeling of humanity, every principle of generosity kindles in my breast, it extinguishes every dirty spark of malice and envy which are but too apt to infest me. I grasp every creature in the arms of universal benevolence and equally participate in the pleasures of the happy and sympathise with the miseries of the unfortunate.

I assure you, my dear, I often look up to the Divine Disposer of events with an eye of gratitude for the blessing which I hope he intends to bestow on me in bestowing you. I mainly wish that he may bless my endeavours to make your life as comfortable and happy as possible, both in sweetening the rougher parts of my natural temper and bettering the unkindly circumstances of my fortune. This, my dear, is a passion, at least in my view, worthy of a man, and I will add, worthy of a Christian. The sordid earth-worm may profess love to a woman's person, whilst in reality his affection is centered on her pocket, and the slavish drudge may go a-wooing as he goes to the horse-market to choose one who is stout and firm, and as we may say of an old horse, one who will be a good drudge and draw kindly. I disdain their dirty puny ideas. I would be heartily out of humour with myself if I thought I were capable of having so poor a notion of the sex which were designed to crown the pleasures of society! Poor devils! I don't envy them their happiness, who have such notions. For my part, I propose quite other pleasures with my dear partner.

R. B.

Madame Charles (Julie Bouchaud de Hérettes) to Alphonse Marie Louis de Prat de Lamartine (1817)

Is it you, Alphonse, is it indeed you, whom I have just pressed in my arms, and who has escaped me like happiness itself? I ask if it be not a celestial spirit that God sent me, if he will return it to me, if I shall see my dear one again, the angel whom I adore! Ah! I must hope so. The same heaven covers us to-day, and from to-night I am sure it will protect us. But cruel people have separated us; what harm they have done us, Alphonse! What have we in common with them, that they should intervene and say: "You are not to look on each other any more!" This block of ice placed on our hearts, has it not afflicted you, oh, my angel? I still feel the cold. I imagined that I went and said to them: "Ah! leave me alone! You must see that I am not in sympathy with you, that I have suffered much, and that if I am to live, he alone must possess my heart!"

They went away, but you could have remained, and I was all alone; why, Alphonse, should we be alarmed? Ah! why not let us bless this Divine Providence? Again to-morrow—is it not so?—she will reunite us, and this time she will leave us together! It is a proof that she still wishes us to submit. But she does not want us to die to-night, and hence must she not receive our complete adoration? I felt this so strongly that, when they left, my first care was to throw myself upon my knees and to worship with tears this supreme Goodness, who has given me Alphonse. Only at God's feet did I recover sufficient strength to speak to His very self. He allows me to love you, Alphonse! I am sure of it! If He forbade it, would He let the fierce love which consumes me go on increasing day by day? Would He permit us to see each other again? Would He have poured upon us, without stint, the treasures of His goodness, and then angrily taken them away? Ah! no, heaven is just. It rebuked us; it will not ruthlessly separate us. Shall I not love you as it wills—as a son, as an angel, as a brother? And you, you, dear child, have you not long promised to see in me nought but your mother?

Ah! how the night flies, how it tortures me! Alphonse, I am not wrong, you are indeed here! We are together; but I shall only be sure of it to-morrow. I must see you again, in order to believe my happiness a reality! Tonight I am too much afflicted.—Dear Valley of Aix! It was not thus that you brought us together; you were not a miser with your heavenly joys! They last like our love, eternal, limitless! All life long they would have endured! Now see them already troubled. But no matter what the time, we should be very wrong, dear child, not to hope for better things!

You will see how constantly I am alone. To-morrow, my angel, if God is good enough to let us live until the evening, you will see how time will fly, unless someone separates us! With you here, you will see whether I complain of my position. Unfortunately, I shall not be free to-morrow until half-past twelve. I am going to the Palace of Justice with M. Charles, to fulfill some formality or other, and I shall leave home at half-past eleven. I think that this will take me an hour. Await me at your place, my angel! I shall be there if I can get away, and I shall get you to take me out, so that we can pass the remainder of the day together. Let us pray God that, until then, He may give us life and strength.

Robert Browning to Elizabeth B. Barrett
(1846)

You will only expect a few words—what will those be? When the heart is full it may run over, but the real fulness stays within.

You asked me yesterday "if I should repent?" Yes—my own Ba,—I could wish all the past were to do over again, that in it I might somewhat more,—never so little more, conform in the outward homage to the inward feeling. What I have professed... (for I have performed nothing) seems to fall short of what my first love required even—and when I think of *this* moment's love... I could repent, as I say.

Words can never tell you, however,—form them, transform them anyway,—how perfectly dear you are to me—perfectly dear to my heart and soul.

I look back, and in every one point, every word and gesture, every letter, every *silence*—you have been entirely perfect to me—I would not change one word, one look.

My hope and aim are to preserve this love, not to fall from it—for which I trust to God who procured it for me, and doubtlessly can preserve it.

Enough now, my dearest, dearest, own Ba! You have given me the highest, completest proof of love that ever one human being gave another. I am all gratitude—and all pride (under the proper feeling which ascribes pride to the right source) all pride that my life has been so crowned by you.

God bless you prays your very own R.

I will write to-morrow of course. Take every care of *my life* which is in that dearest little hand; try and be composed, my beloved.

ADORING
LOVE

Henry VIII to Anne Boleyn
(ca. 1528?)

On considering in my mind the contents of your last letters, I have put myself into great agony, not knowing how to interpret them, whether to my disadvantage, as you show in some places, or to my advantage, as I understand them in some others, beseeching you earnestly to let me know expressly your whole mind as to the love between us two.

It is necessary for me to obtain this answer, having been for above a whole year stricken with the dart of love, and not yet sure whether I shall fail of finding a place in your heart and affection, which last point has prevented me for some time past from calling you my mistress; for, if you only love me with an ordinary love, that name is not suitable for you, because it denotes a singular love, which is far from common. But if you please to do the office of a true, loyal mistress and friend, and to give up yourself body and heart to me, who will be, and have been, your most loyal servant, if your rigour does not forbid me, I promise you that not only the name shall be given you, but also that I will take you for my only mistress, casting off all others besides you out of my thoughts and affections, and serve you only.

I beseech you to give an entire answer to this my rude letter, that I may know on what and how far I may depend. And if it does not please you to answer me in writing, appoint some place where I may have it by word of mouth, and I will go thither with all my heart. No more, for fear of tiring you.

Written by the hand of him who would willingly remain yours,

H. R.

Margaret of Valois to James, Lord of Chanvallon
(ca. 1580?)

Our passions and our longings are so much in sympathy one with the other, my dear heart, that we ought to believe that the same soul throbs in our two bodies, that love of the same character possesses our hearts, and that fate, envious of our union, rears up to oppose our ecstasy and destroy our contentment.

This thought helps me to support my misfortunes, since all the philosophy of love is summed up in the idea that what afflicts one should afflict the other, and that each should suffer with the other. And so, all obstacles count as drops of water on my flame. Absence, the petty things of the day, the inconveniences of life, cause my love to grow, albeit a weak soul and a craven heart would give way before their persecution.

I retired yesterday before the evening dancing began, and my chamber was full of all the gallants of the court. Such a diversion, which would have shocked any other passion, had the same effect on mine that waves make on an immovable rock. I arose early to behold the beautiful day, to feel the cool of the morning, and to see how the flowers of nature are so far superior to the flowers of the court, as gods are above men. In my thought and action I allow myself to be susceptible of only those things that nourish my love, which I cherish and preserve as the true strength and breath of my life, which, giving itself ever anew to you, oh, beauteous one, is consecrated unto all eternity.

Farewell, fair sun, farewell, beautiful angel and beauteous miracle of nature, I kiss a million times the myriads of perfections which the gods have given you for men to admire.

Henry of Navarre to Gabriella D'Estrées
(1594)

I write to you, dear heart, from the foot of your picture, which I adore only because it was made for you, not because it resembles you. I may consider myself a good judge since I have you engraven, with all your perfections, in my soul, in my heart, and in my eyes.

Endymion Porter to His Wife, Olive
(ca.1622?)

My dearest Olive,

Thy care in sending to me shows me how truly thou lovest me, and thy fear of my inconstancy argues no want of affection, only of faith, which, if any good works of mine may strengthen, I will come on my knees to see thee, and put out my eyes rather than look with unchaste desire upon any creature while I breathe; and to be more secure of me, I would have thee inquire if ever I was false to any *friend*, and then to consider what a traitor I should be, if to a wife (and to such a wife!) so virtuous and good, I should prove false, and not to my friends. Dear Olive, be assured that I strive to make myself happy in nothing but in thee, and therefore I charge you to be merry, and to cherish your health and life, the more because I live in you. But what can I say, or what in the least little can I do? *Love you?* That I do and ever shall, as he who vows never to be anybody's but your true husband.

ENDYMION PORTER

William Congreve to Mrs. Arabella Hunt
(ca. 1690?)

Dear Madam,

This I send by the permission of a severe father, I will not say a cruel one, since he is yours. What is it that he has taken so mortally ill of me? That I die for his daughter is my only offence. And yet he has refused to let me take ev'n my farewell of you. Thrice happy be the omen! May I never take my farewell of thee till my soul takes leave of my body; at least he cannot restrain me from loving; no, I will love thee in spite of all opposition.

Tho' your friends and mine prove equally averse, yet I will love thee with a constancy which shall appear to all the world to have something noble in it, that all the world shall confess that it deserved not to be unfortunate.

I will forsake even my friends for thee, my honest, my witty, my brave friends, who had always been, till I had seen thee, the dearest part of mankind to me. Thou shalt supply the place of them all with me; thou shalt be my bosom, my best-lov'd friend, and at the same time my only mistress and my dearest wife.

Have the goodness to pardon this familiarity, 'tis the tenderest leave of the faithfulest lover, and here to show an over respectfulness would be to wrong my passion. That I love thee more than life, nay, even than glory, which I once courted with a burning desire, bear witness all my unquiet days, and every restless night, and that terrible agitation of mind and body which proceeded from my fear of losing thee. To lose thee is to lose all happiness: tormenting reflection to a sensible soul! How often has my reason been going upon it? But the loss of reason would be but too happy upon the loss of thee, since all the advantage that I could draw from its presence would be to know myself miserable.

But the time calls upon me; I am obliged to take an odious journey, and leave thee behind with my enemies. But thine shall never do thee harm with me. Adieu, thou dearest, thou loveliest of creatures! No change of time or place, or the remonstrances of the best of friends, shall ever be able to alter my passion for thee. Be but one quarter so kind, so just to me, and the sun will not shine on a happier man than myself.

Lord Peterborough to Henrietta Howard
(ca. 1722?)

By my honour, by truth, which I love almost as well as the author of my torments,—I protest to you there is a lady so terrible to me that the first moments I approach her I can hardly speak! And I feel myself the greatest fool in nature near the woman in the world who has the most wit.

To what has a friend innocently exposed me? The brims of the cup were sweet, but the dose was strong, and I drank it down with too much greediness. What I may obtain, I know not; what I have lost, I know—in a word: all satisfaction and my quiet; and I remain tasteless to all pleasures, and to all of your sex but one.

But I expect little by this account from the person in question. I believe it is not new to her to see such effects of her wit and beauty, and I fear she may have hardened her heart by the knowledge of her superior worth, and by a just contempt of mankind. Alas! were there some differences betwixt my adoration and that of others, how shall I make it known? Some angry deity, designing punishment, gave to one woman so many different charms; and I was fated to be the wretched man capable of receiving as much love as he could give.

Dennis Diderot to Sophie Volland
(1759)

You are well! You think of me! You love me. You will always love me. I believe you: now am I happy. I live again: I can talk, work, play, walk— do anything you wish. I must have made myself very disagreeable the last two or three days. No! my love; your very presence would not have delighted me more than your first letter did. How impatiently I waited for it! I am sure my hands trembled when opening it. My countenance changed; my voice altered; and unless he were a fool, he who handed it to me would have said—"That man receives news from his father or mother, or some one else he loves." I was just at that moment about to send you a letter expressing my great uneasiness. While you are amusing yourself, you forget how much my heart suffers. . . . Adieu, my dearest love. My affection for you is ardent and sincere. I would love you even more than I do, if I knew how.

Marquis de Lafayette to His Wife, Madame de Lafayette
(1777)

I send you an open letter, my dearest love, by M. de Valfort, my friend, whom I beg you will receive as such. He will tell you at length everything concerning me; but I must tell you myself how well I love you. I have too much pleasure in experiencing this sentiment not to have also pleasure in repeating it to you a thousand times, if that were possible. I have no resource left me, my love, but to write and write again, without even hoping that my letters will ever reach you, and I endeavour to console myself, by the pleasure of conversing with you, for the pain and disappointment of not receiving a single line from France. It is impossible to describe to you how completely my heart is torn by anxiety and fear; nor should I wish to express all I feel, even if it were in my power to do so; for I would not disturb, by any mournful impressions, the happiest moments of my exile—those in which I can speak to you of my affection.

But do you, at least, pity me? Do you understand all that I endure? If I could only know at this moment where you are, and what you are doing! But in the course of time I shall learn all this, for I am not separated from you in reality, as if I were dead. I am expecting your letters with an impatience, from which nothing can for an instant divert my thoughts: everyone tells me they must soon arrive: but can I rely on it? Neglect not one opportunity of writing to me, if my happiness be still dear to you. Repeat to me that you love me: the less I merit your affection, the more necessary to me are your consoling assurances of it.

Robert Burns to Ellison Begbie
(1780)

My dear E.,

I do not remember, in the course of your acquaintance and mine, ever to have heard your opinion on the ordinary way of falling in love, amongst people of our station of life—I do not mean the persons who proceed in the way of bargain, but those whose affection is really placed on the person.

Though I be, as you know very well, but a very awkward lover myself, yet, as I have some opportunities of observing the conduct of others who are much better skilled in the affair of courtship than I am, I often think it is owing to lucky chance more than to good management that there are not more unhappy marriages than usually are.

It is natural for a young fellow to like the acquaintance of the females, and customary for him to keep their company when occasion serves. Some one of them is more agreeable to him than the rest; there is something—he knows not what—pleases him—he knows not how—in her company. This I take to be what is called *love* with the greater part of us; and I must own, my dear E., it is a hard game, such a one as you have to play when you meet with such a lover. You cannot admit but he is sincere; and yet, though you use him ever so favourably, perhaps in a few months, or, at farthest, a year or two, the same unaccountable fancy may make him as distractedly fond of another, whilst you are quite forgot. I am aware that perhaps the next time I have the pleasure of seeing you you may bid me take my own lesson home, and tell me that the passion I have professed for you is perhaps one of those transient flashes I have been describing; but I hope, my dear E., you will do me the justice to believe me when I assure you that the love I have for you is founded on the sacred principles of virtue and honour; and, by consequence, so long as you continue possessed of those amiable qualities which first inspired my passion for you, so long must I continue to love you. Believe me, my dear, it is love like this alone which can render the married state happy. People may talk of flames and raptures as long as they please, and a warm fancy, with a flow of youthful spirits, may make them feel something like what they describe; but sure am I, the nobler faculties of the mind, with kindred feelings of the heart, can only be the foundation of friendship; and it has always been my opinion that the married life is only *friendship* in a more exalted degree.

If you will be so good as to grant my wishes, and it should please Providence to spare us to the latest periods of life, I can look forward and see that even then, though bent down with wrinkled age,—even then, when all other worldly circumstances will be indifferent to me, I will regard my E. with the tenderest affection,—and for this plain reason, because she is still possessed of those noble qualities, improved to a much higher degree, which first inspired my affection for her.

> O happy state, when souls each other draw,
> Where love is liberty, and nature law.

I know, were I to speak in such a style to many a girl who thinks herself possessed of no small share of sense, she would think it ridiculous; but the language of the heart is, my dear E., the only courtship I shall ever use to you.

When I look over what I have written I am sensible it is vastly different from the ordinary style of courtship; but I make no apology. I know your good nature will excuse what your good sense may see amiss.

Friedrich von Schiller to Charlotte von Lengenfeld (1789)

It is true, dearest Lotte? Am I to hope that Caroline read in your soul, and answered from your heart what I did not dare to confess? Oh, how hard it has been for me to keep this secret, which I was obliged to do from the beginning of our acquaintance! Often, while we were living together, I summoned up all my courage, and went to you with the intention of disclosing the truth—but that courage always deserted me. I thought I discovered selfishness in my wishes; I feared that I was taking none but my own happiness into account, and this it was that deterred me. If I could not be as much to you as you were to me, my grief would have saddened you, and I should have spoiled the beautiful harmony of our friendship by my avowal, should have lost what I had already gained— your pure sisterly affection. Yet there were moments when my hopes rose, when the happiness we might give each other seemed superior to all earthly considerations, when I even believed it would be a noble act to sacrifice everything else to that felicity. You might be happy without me—but you should never be unhappy because of me. This I felt most irresistibly—and upon this I built my hopes. You might give yourself to another, but no one would love you more reverently and tenderly than I. To no one would your happiness mean more than it did and always will to me.

My whole existence, everything that lives within me, everything, my dearest, do I devote to you; and if I am trying to become a better man, I am doing so to become more and more worthy of you, and to gladden your days more and more. Excellence of soul is a beautiful and indestructible bond of friendship and of love. Our friendship and our love will never be destroyed, and will last for all time—like the feelings upon which they are founded.

Forget everything now that might put a restraint upon your heart, and allow your emotions free speech. Confirm what Caroline let me understand I could hope for. Tell me you will be mine, and that to kiss me will cost you not a single sacrifice. Oh, assure me of this with one little word! Our hearts have long been near together; anything that may be between us, let it drop now, so that nought may disturb the free communication of our souls.

Farewell, dearest Lotte. I long for a quiet moment in which to describe to you all the feelings that in all this time have made me so joyful and miserable in turn. Oh, how much I have to tell you! Do not tarry to banish my anxiety for ever. I place my whole life's felicity in your hands. Good-bye, my dearest.

Napoleon Bonaparte to His Wife, Josephine
(1796)

My waking thoughts are all of you. Your portrait and the remembrance of last night's delirium have robbed my senses of repose. Sweet and incomparable Josephine, what an extraordinary influence you have over my heart. Are you vexed, do I see you sad, are you ill at ease? My soul is broken with grief, and there is no rest for your lover. But is there more for me when, giving ourselves up to the deep feelings which master me, I breathe out upon your lips, upon your heart, a flame which burns me up—ah, it was this past night I realised that your portrait was not you. I start at noon; I shall see you in three hours. Meanwhile, *mio dolce amor*, accept a thousand kisses, but give me none, for they fire my blood.

N. B.

Ludwig van Beethoven to "Immortal Beloved"
(Countess Theresa von Brunswick)
(1806)

My angel—my all—myself—only a few words to-day, and those with a lead pencil, too, (with thine)—my stay here is only certain until to-morrow—what a contemptible waste of time and everything else— but why this deep sorrow when necessity speaks—can our love exist otherwise than through sacrifices, it cannot attain everything, canst thou change it, that thou art not entirely mine. I entirely thine? Ah! look into the beautiful nature, and calm thy spirit about what is inevitable.— Love demands everything, and justly, too, so it is with thee, thee with me—but do not lightly forget that I must live for myself and for thee—if we were not so entirely united—thou would perceive this pain as little as I.... We will, perhaps, see each other soon, but I cannot tell you my thoughts now, which I have had regarding my life, during these days—if our hearts were only always close together! I cannot imagine anything as beautiful as that, the heart has much to tell you—ah! there are moments when I find that language is in vain. Comfort thy spirit, remain ever my true, only treasure, my all, as I am thine. The rest, what is to be for us, and what shall be, the gods must send....

Ah! where am I, art thou with me! For thee and me I will work, so that I can live with thee; what a life! So!!! without thee, persecuted by the kindness of certain men—a kindness I do not and will not merit— humility from man to man pains me, and when I consider myself in connection with the universe what am I, and what is He whom we call the Greatest? And still therein lies the divinity of man.

I weep when I think that at the earliest, it will probably be Saturday when thou receivest the first news from me,—also how thou lovest me. But I love thee more; never conceal thy thoughts from me. Good night! being here for my health I must go to bed early. Oh! God, so near, and so far! Are not our lives truly a heavenly mansion, and as strong as the vault of heaven?

Bettina Brentano to Johann Wolfgang von Goethe
(ca. 1807?)

Thou knowest my heart; thou knowest that all there is desire, thought, boding, and longing; thou livest among spirits, and they give thee divine wisdom. Thou must nourish me; thou givest all that in advance which I do not understand to ask. My mind has a small compass, my love a large one; thou must bring them to a balance. Love cannot be quiet till the mind matches its growth; thou art matched to my love; thou art friendly, kind, indulgent: let me know when my heart is off the balance. I understand thy silent signs.

A look from thy eyes into mine, a kiss from thee upon my lips, instructs me in all that seems delightful to learn from such sweet experience. I am far from thee; kisses are become strange to me. I ever return in thought to that hour when thou heldest me in the soft enfoldment of thine arm. Then I begin to weep; but tears dry unawares. Yes, he reaches with his love (thus do I muse) over to me in this still retreat; and should not I, with my eternal, unceasing longing, reach to him in the distance? Ah, conceive what my heart has to say to thee. It overflows with soft sighs, and they all whisper to thee. May my only happiness on earth be thy friendliness to me. Oh, dear friend! give me but a sign that thou art conscious of me!

Lord Byron to the Countess Guccioli
(1819)

My Dearest Teresa,

I have read this book in your garden; my love, you were absent, or else I could not have read it. It is a favourite book of yours, and the writer was a friend of mine. You will not understand these English words, and *others* will not understand them,—which is the reason I have not scrawled them in Italian. But you will recognize the handwriting of him who passionately loved you, and you will divine that, over a book which was yours, he could only think of love. In that word, beautiful in all languages, but most so in yours—*Amor mio*—is comprised my existence here and hereafter. I feel I exist here, and I fear that I shall exist hereafter,— to *what* purpose you will decide; my destiny rests with you, and you are a woman, eighteen years of age, and two out of a convent. I wish that you had stayed there, with all my heart,—or, at least, that I had never met you in your married state.

But all this is too late. I love you, and you love me,—at least, you *say* so, and *act* as if you *did* so, which last is a great consolation in all events. But *I* more than love you, and cannot cease to love you.

Think of me, sometimes, when the Alps and the ocean divide us,— but they never will, unless you *wish* it.

BYRON

Edward Bulwer Lytton to Rosina Wheeler (1826)

I have twice begun to write, and twice I have destroyed what I have written—the same restraint which oppressed me in speaking, seems to operate also upon this method of uttering the feelings you have inspired. No matter! Their *nature* you have discovered. Love, admiration, passion, are not the less deeply felt for being imperfectly expressed; the trembling of the voice, the embarrassment of manner, the difficulty of expression which diminish the *eloquence*, do justice at least to the reality of feeling.

From the first moment I saw you, I was attracted towards you. The sentiments you inspired carried me back to years of more fresh and unsullied remembrance. They had no place among the ordinary attach-ments which the world had more lately afforded me. I could not define their nature; I could not reason them away. Early circumstances, which embittered and darkened my character, the exhaustion of feeling which follows an over-wrought excitation, and that premature acquaintance with the world which tends above all things to harden the heart, had brought me the great lesson of time, had learnt me to reduce affection into a system, and to despise passion as the sickliness of romance. "None are so desolate, but something dear" will at times relieve and brighten the monotony of our progress through life; but if, of late years, I have formed attachments, they have been made by circumstances, and they found but a feeble echo in the heart. It was you who taught me that my first and deepest emotions were smothered—not extinct. It was you who discovered to me the truth of experience had something in store for me still more precious than the creations of Fancy, and that my earliest visions of Beauty and Love never equalled the perfection I beheld and coveted in *you*. I came here,—in proportion as I saw more of you, I discovered more clearly the nature of your sentiments to me.

Let me here digress for an instant, and confess to you the earliest,— the prevailing, the most yearning weakness of my nature. It is, to find in the one who should become to me the most dear, feelings not only not dissimilar in their *nature*, but in their extent, to those I should experience myself. I cannot love *truly*, without loving with that earnestness and devotion of thought and soul which I feel no ordinary attachment could repay. Does this seem to you vanity? Believe me that it is not so. I felt as if I should never meet such a return, and I therefore shrunk from such depth of feeling in myself.

Years have passed since I experienced any emotion like that which I feel for you at this moment. Better, perhaps, for me, if I had still been successful in subduing my heart. I return to my subject. I came here—a spell was upon me—I dared not express to you what I felt. I talked with levity in order to obtain an escape from the more serious subjects in which Feeling is engaged—I could not trust myself with those. I said that I discovered the nature of your sentiments to me. I saw that there was not one of the nature which could alone satisfy my heart, and I should have left you with my own unuttered (at least by the lips), and with the resolution to forget you, had not all the coldness of previous reflection been destroyed yesterday by the imprudence of a single moment; I touched you, I held your hand in mine, and I felt as if you alone were all the world. What were Reason, Resolution, the wisdom of Premeditation, to the impulse of that unguarded instant? I saw then it was due to you to express myself more clearly. I did so. Oh, God! would that in that brief but memorable conversation which ensued, I could have overcome the chilling impression that, even amid the gentleness and kindness of your manner, my feelings were unshared. Yet what could I expect? A mind and heart like yours are not lightly won, and yet I had left nothing to Time. I told you that I adored you; I repeat it. Examine your own feelings, and tell me candidly what I may dare to expect. I do not ask if the sensations I would excite are awakened; I only ask if they are capable of being so. For the happiness of both of us, answer me this from your very heart.

I have disclosed to you the great, the perhaps unreasonable, return which my own requires; consider *that*, when you give me your reply. I turn from the feelings I experience to the circumstances under which I am placed.

I am my mother's favourite son. I was brought up solely by her, when my brothers spent their childhood chiefly with other relations. She considers me, therefore, as the one whose fate will more immediately reflect upon her, and perhaps for that reason she is particularly ambitious respecting it. Her affection makes her desire that I should be happy, but her pride that I should find my happiness in the distinctions of the world. As yet I have been indifferent to these, for I have no object in obtaining them; and it is from despair at my indolence that my mother has wished that my marriage at least should, as it is termed, advance me in the world. Under present circumstances, I feel too well that she would not give her consent to a marriage which, while she acknowledged it as most honourable, would still appear to her imprudent! But it is only under present circumstances. If I had once attained the distinction she desires for me, Fortune and Connection in marriage would cease to be an object. She has even told me (and I know her generosity and kindness too well to disbelieve it) that I might then consult my happiness according to my own ideas; and when no longer biased by a previous prejudice, she would perceive and acknowledge what reason she would have for pride and exultation in that connection which is the first desire of my Heart.

I said that I had no object in earning reputation. Suffer me, my beautiful and adored Friend, to desire it from *you*—tell me for *your sake* to exert myself, and from that instant a new spirit shall possess me. What could I not hope for, what could I not achieve, if your smile was my inspiration and your love my reward? I do not speak from the romance of a momentary impulse, or the too sanguine expectations of an inexperienced ambition. Hard as it is for persons depressed by poverty and birth to obtain distinction, to those in a more fortunate situation it requires little but the stimulus and exertion. Tell me to hope for *you*, Rosina, and every other object of ambition will appear easy and mean in comparison.

Helmuth von Moltke to Mary Burt
(1842)

Let us always be quite sincere with one another, and on no account sulk. Better to quarrel than that; but best of all to live quite in harmony. I dare say you have noticed that I am sometimes moody. Just leave me alone on those occasions; I shall be sure to come back to you. I will, however, take pains to improve. From you I wish good humour and even spirits, and when possible a cheerful *temper*, compliance in trifles, orderly housekeeping, neatness in dress, and above all things that you go on loving me. It is true that you are very young to enter a totally new sphere of surroundings; but your good sense, and above all the excellence of your disposition will soon make you at home in inter-course with other people. Be persuaded, dear Mary, that kindness to everyone is the first rule of life, and saves us much trouble, and that it is possible to be on good terms even with people whom you do not like, without insincerity or want of good faith. The natural friendliness of a kind heart is true courtesy and the finest polish. In my case bad bringing up and a youth of privations often choked this feeling, and still oftener checked its utterance, and so now I have but the acquired coldness of a haughty courtesy, which seldom attracts anyone. You, on the contrary, are young and pretty, and will not, God willing, know any privation; everyone will treat you with cordiality. Do not, then, omit to be amiable to people in return, and to make friends of them. This to a large extent, of course, depends on your conversation. There is no question at all of saying anything witty, but when possible say something kind, and if that is not possible at least let it be felt that you would like to do so. You are quite without affectation and insincerity; that sort of thing wearies one directly, for nothing but truth can arouse sympathy. Real modesty and absence of pretension are the true protection against annoyances and mortifications in the great world, and I may almost affirm that with these qualities shyness and awkwardness are out of the question. If we do not try to appear other than we are, and to usurp a higher position than becomes us, neither rank nor birth nor numbers and display can discompose us. But if man has no inward consciousness of his worth, and is obliged to seek it in the opinion of others, he has always to read the eyes of strangers, just like one who wears false hair, and has to look in every glass to see that nothing has gone wrong.

I confess, dear Mary, that I draw these fine lessons from myself. My manners are nothing but shyness varnished over with self-confidence and *usage du monde*. The many years of repression in which I grew up have permanently injured my character, suppressed my feelings, and stifled right and proper pride. It was not until late in life that I began to build up again from within what had not been destroyed. Do you help me, then, from now on to improve. You yourself, however, I should like to see nobler and better—which is the same thing as being happier and more contented—than I can now become. So be modest and unpretending, and you will have a calm mind and entire ease.

I shall be glad to see people paying due court to you, and I have no objection to a little coquetry. The better terms you are on with everybody, the less opportunity people will have for saying of you that you favour individuals. You must be cautious on this score, for men seek to please, first for the sake of pleasing, and then that they may boast of it, and you will find far more captiousness than charity in Society. It is certain that I shall very often fall short of other men whom you will see here. At every ball you will find some who dance better and dress better, and at every party some whose conversation is livelier, and who are better-tempered than I. But your discovering this need not prevent your still loving me best, provided only that you believe that I care more for you than for anyone else. Whenever something should happen that you cannot tell me, then be on your guard against yourself. And now, give me a kiss, and I will have done with lecturing. I am glad that little Ernestine is now well again, and that little Henry is thriving. Love to mamma and papa.

One thing more, dear Mary. When you are writing just read the letter you are answering through again. It is not only the questions that require to be answered, but it is well to touch upon every topic mentioned in it. Otherwise the exchange of letters grows more and more meagre, mutual ground vanishes, and people soon reach the point of only caring to communicate what is important. Now, life consists for the most part of small and unimportant matters. The little affairs of every day range themselves into hours, weeks, and months, and in the end make up the happiness and sorrow of life. That is why real intercourse is so much better than correspondence. People tell one another the merest trifles, but have a difficulty in finding what seems worth the trouble of writing about.

Heinrich Heine to the "Fly" (Elise Krinitz)
(1856)

Dear Child,

My best wishes to you for the new year. This box may not be to your taste, but I hope the chocolates will be. I dare say you will attach little importance to my thus complying with the observances prescribed by custom; but we must not allow any of our acquaintances to imagine there might be a want of esteem between us. So we must not neglect these little conventional formalities. Really, I love you so much that I see no need for esteem at all. You are my dear Fly. And my sufferings seem less oppressive when I think of your sweetness and the charm of your company.

Edgar Allan Poe to Mrs. Sarah Helen Whitman
(1848)

I have already told you that some few casual words spoken of you by —— ——, were the first in which I had ever heard your name mentioned. She alluded to what she called your "eccentricities," and hinted at your sorrows. Her description of the former strangely arrested—her allusion to the latter enchained and rivetted my attention.

She had referred to thoughts, sentiments, traits, *moods*, which I knew to be my own, but which, until that moment, I had believed to be my own solely—unshared by any human being. A profound sympathy took immediate possession of my soul. I cannot better explain to you what I felt than by saying that your unknown heart seemed to pass into my bosom—there to dwell for ever—while mine, I thought, was translated into your own.

From that hour I loved you. Since that period I have never seen nor heard your name without a shiver, half of delight, half of anxiety.—The impression left upon my mind was that you were still a wife, and it is only within the last few months that I have been undeceived in this respect.

For this reason I shunned your presence and even the city in which you lived. You may remember that once when I passed through Providence with Mrs. Osgood I positively refused to accompany her to your house, and even provoked her into a quarrel by the obstinacy and seeming unreasonableness of my refusal. I dared neither go nor say why I could not. I dared not speak of you—much less see you. For years your name never passed my lips, while my soul drank in, with a delirious thirst, all that was uttered in my presence respecting you.

The merest whisper that concerned you awoke in me a shuddering sixth sense, vaguely compounded of fear, ecstatic happiness and a wild inexplicable sentiment that resembled nothing so nearly as a conscious-ness of guilt.

Judge, then, with what wondering, unbelieving joy, I received, in your well-known MS., the Valentine which first gave me to see that you knew me to exist.

The idea of what men call Fate lost then in my eyes its character of futility. I felt that nothing hereafter was to be doubted, and lost myself for many weeks in one continuous, delicious dream, where all was a vivid, yet indistinct bliss.—

Immediately after reading the Valentine, I wished to contrive some mode of acknowledging—without wounding you by seeming directly to acknowledge—my sense—oh, my keen—my exulting—my ecstatic sense of the honour you had conferred on me. To accomplish as I wished it, precisely *what* I wished, seemed impossible, however; and I was on the point of abandoning the idea, when my eyes fell upon a volume of my own poems; and then the lines I had written, in my passionate boyhood, to the first purely ideal love of my soul—to the Helen Stannard of whom I told you—flashed upon my recollection. I turned to them. They expressed all—*all* that I would have said to you—so fully—so accurately and so exclusively, that a thrill of intense superstition ran at once through my frame. Read the verses and then take into consideration the peculiar need I had, at the moment, for just so seemingly an unattainable mode of communication with you as they afforded. Think of the absolute appositeness with which they fulfilled that need—expressing not only all that I would have said of your person, but all that I most wished to assure you, in the lines commencing—

On desperate seas long wont to roam.

Think of the rare agreement of name, and you will no longer wonder that to one accustomed as I am to the Calculus of Probabilities, they wore an air of positive miracle. . . . I yielded at once to an overwhelming sense of Fatality. From that hour I have never been able to shake from my soul the belief that my Destiny, for good or for evil, either here or hereafter, is in some measure interwoven with your own.

Of course I did not expect, on your part, any acknowledgment of the printed lines "To Helen"; and yet, without confessing it even to myself, I experienced an indefinable sense of sorrow in your silence. At length, when I thought you had time fully to forget me (if, indeed, you had ever really remembered) I sent you the anonymous lines in MS. I wrote, first, through a pining, burning desire to communicate with you in *some* way—even if you remained in ignorance of your correspondent. The mere thought that *your* dear fingers would press—*your* sweet eyes dwell upon characters which *I* had penned—characters which had welled out upon the paper from the depths of so devout a love—filled my soul with a rapture, which seemed, then, all sufficient for my human nature. It *then* appeared to me that merely this one thought involved so much of bliss that here on earth I could have no right ever to repine—no room for discontent. If ever, *then*, I dared to picture for myself a richer happiness, it was always connected with your image in Heaven. But there was yet another idea which impelled me to send you those lines:—I said to myself the sentiment—the holy passion which glows in my bosom *for her*, is of Heaven, heavenly, and has no taint of the earth. Thus then must lie in the recesses of her own pure bosom, at least the germ of a reciprocal love, and if this be indeed so, she will need no earthly due—she will instinctively feel who is her correspondent—In this case, then, I may hope for some faint token at least, giving me to understand that the source of the poem is known as its sentiment comprehended even if disapproved.

Oh, God!—how long—*how long* I waited in *vain*—hoping against hope—until, at length, I became possessed with a spirit far sterner—far more reckless than despair—I explained to you—but without detailing the vital influence they wrought upon my fortune—the singular additional, yet seemingly trivial fatality by which you happened to address your anonymous stanzas to Fordham instead of New York—by which my aunt happened to get notice of their being in the West Farm post-office. But I have not yet told you that your lines reached me in Richmond on the very day in which I was about to enter on a course which would have borne me far, far away from *you*, sweet, sweet Helen, and from this divine dream of your love.

Claire to Victor Hugo
(1851)

If I were to tell you, my beloved, that since Wednesday I have thought only of you, perhaps you would not believe me; perhaps—but it is the exact truth. I think of you, nothing but you. If I wished to get rid of this thought I don't think I could do so. I say I don't think, but I have not tried to do so, nor ever will. I am so happy when I think of you. To read your verses and think of you is my only happiness. And see, you occupy my thoughts so much that I not only think of you by day but dream of you at night. I am very glad it is so, and hope you also think of me a little, a little or much or even *too much*.

Everything passed off well on Wednesday. They did not send to look for me, and on my return in time I thought of doing the same thing again. In a fortnight, I hope, I shall see you again, and this thought makes me very happy.

You told me, my poet, that when you are with me you lose your memory. Well, it's exactly the same with me. I only think of looking at you and listening to your voice; I forget what I wanted to ask you or say to you. I do not even tell you how much I admire you, how much I love you, how often I think of you. But you know that very well, don't you? And then, when I am no longer with you, my memory comes back. I see all I forgot, and say I was very stupid that I did not profit by the time I had spent with you; but it is then too late, and another time it will be the same.

MARRIED
LOVE

Anne Winthrop to Her Husband, Adam Winthrop
(ca. 1572?)

I have received (right dear and well-beloved) from you this week a letter, though short, yet very sweet, which gave me a lively taste of those sweet and comfortable words which always, when you be present with me, are wont to flow most abundantly from your loving heart,—whereby I perceive that whether you be present with me or absent from me, you are ever one towards me, and your heart remaineth always with me. Wherefore, laying up this persuasion of you in my breast, I will most assuredly, the Lord assisting me by his grace, bear always the like loving heart unto you again, until such time as I may more fully enjoy your loving presence; but in the meantime I will remain as one having a great inheritance, or rich treasure, and it being by force kept from him, or he being in a strange country and cannot enjoy it, longeth continually after it, sighing and sorrowing that he is so long bereft of it, yet rejoiceth that he hath so great treasure pertaining to him, and hopeth that one day the time will come that he shall enjoy it and have the whole benefit of it. So I, having a good hope of the time to come, do more patiently bear the time present, and I pray send me word if you be in health, and what success you have with your letters.

Sir Walter Raleigh to His Wife, Lady Raleigh
(1603)

You shall now receive, dear wife, my last words in these my last lines. My love I send you, that you may keep it when I am dead; and my counsel, that you may remember it when I am no more. I would not by my will present you with sorrows, dear Bess; let them go to the grave, and be buried with me in dust. And seeing it is not the will of God that I shall ever see you more in this life, bear it patiently and with a heart like thyself.

Firstly, I send you all the thanks my heart can conceive, or my words can express, for your many troubles and cares taken for me; which, though they have not taken effect as you wished, yet the debt stands none the less, and pay it I never shall in this world.

Secondly, I beseech you by the love you bare me living, do not hide yourself in grief many days, but seek to help the miserable fortunes of our poor child. Thy mourning cannot avail me; I am but dust.... Remember your poor child for his father's sake, who chose and loved you in his happiest time. God is my witness it is for *you* and *yours* I desired life; but it is true I disdain myself for begging of it. For know, dear wife, that your son is the son of a true man, and one who in his own respect despiseth death, and all his misshapen grisly forms. I cannot write much. God knows how hardly I stole the time, when all sleep; and it is time to separate my thoughts from the world. Beg my dead body, which living is denied thee, and either lay it at Sherbourne or in Exeter, by my father and mother. I can write no more. Time and death call me away.

The everlasting God, Infinite, Powerful, Inscrutable, the Almighty God, which is Goodness itself, Mercy itself, the true light and life, keep thee and thine, have mercy on me, and teach me to forgive my perse-cutors and false witnesses, and send us to meet again in His Glorious Kingdom. My own true wife, farewell. Bless my poor boy. Pray for me, and let the good God fold you both in His arms.

Written with the dying hand of sometime thy husband, but now, alas! overthrown.

Yours that was, but not now my own,

W. RALEIGH

Richard Steele to His Wife, Mary
(1714)

Dear Madam,

If great obligations received are just motives for addresses of this kind, you have an unquestionable pretension to my acknowledgments who have condescended to give me your very self. I can make no return for so inestimable a favour, but in acknowledging the generosity of the giver. To have either wealth, wit, or beauty is generally a temptation to a woman to put an unreasonable value upon herself; but with all these in a degree which drew upon you the addresses of men of the amplest fortunes, you bestowed yourself where you could have no expectations but from the gratitude of the receiver, though you knew he could exert that gratitude in no other returns but esteem and love. For which must I first thank you,—for what you have denied yourself or what you have bestowed upon me?

I owe to you, that for my sake you have overlooked the prospect of living in pomp and plenty, and I have not been circumspect enough to preserve you from care and sorrow. I will not dwell upon this particular: you are so good a wife that I know you think I rob you of more than I can give, when I say anything in your favour to my own disadvantage. Whoever should see or hear you, would think it were worth leaving all in the world for you; while I, habitually possessed of that happiness, have been throwing away important endeavours for the rest of mankind, to the neglect of her, for whom every other man in his senses would be apt to sacrifice everything else.

I know not by what unreasonable prepossession it is, but methinks there must be something austere to give authority to wisdom, and I cannot account for having only rallied many reasonable sentiments of yours, but that you are too beautiful to appear judicious. One may grow fond, but not wise, from what is said by so lovely a counsellor. Hard fate, that you have been lessened by your perfections, and lost power by your very charms.

That ingenuous spirit in all your behaviour, that familiar grace in your words and actions, has for these seven years only inspired admiration and love. But experience has taught me, the best counsel I ever have received has been pronounced by the fairest and softest lips, and convinced me that in you I am blessed with a wise friend, as well as a charming mistress.

Your mind shall no longer suffer by your person; nor shall your eyes for the future dazzle me into a blindness towards your understanding. I rejoice, in this public manner, to show my esteem for you, and must do you the justice to say that there can be no virtue represented in all this collection for the female world, which I have not known you exert as far as the opportunities of your fortune have given you leave. Forgive me, that my heart overflows with love and gratitude for daily instances of your prudent economy, the just disposition you make of your little affairs, your cheerfulness in dispatch of them, your prudent forbearance of any reflection that they might have needed less vigilance if you had disposed of your fortune more suitably; in short, for all the arguments you every day give me of a generous and sincere affection.

It is impossible for me to look back on many evils and pains which I have suffered since we came together, without a pleasure which is not to be expressed, from the proofs I have had in these circumstances of your unwearied goodness. How often has your tenderness removed pain from my sick head! how often anguish from my afflicted heart! With how skilful patience have I known you comply with the vain projects which pain has suggested, to have an aching limb removed by journeying from one side of the room to another! how often, the next instant, travelled the same ground again, without telling your patient it was to no purpose to change his situation! If there are such beings as guardian angels, thus are they employed. I will no more believe one of them more good in its inclinations, than I can conceive it more charming in form than my wife.

But I offend, and forget what I write to you is to appear in public. You are so great a lover of home that I know it will be irksome to you to go into the world, even in an applause. I will end this without so much as mentioning your little flock, or your own amiable figure at the head of it. That I think them preferable to all other children I know is the effect of passion and instinct; that I believe you the best of wives I know proceeds from experience and reason.

I am, Madam, your most obliged husband and most obedient, humble servant,

RICHARD STEELE

Marquis de Lafayette to His Wife, Madame de Lafayette (1777)

I am each day more miserable from having quit you, my dearest love; I hope to receive news from you at Philadelphia, and this hope adds much to the impatience I feel to arrive in that city.

Farewell, my life; I am in such haste that I know not what I write, but I do know that I love you more tenderly than ever, that the pain of this separation was necessary to convince me how very dear you are to me, and that I would give at this moment half my existence for the pleasure of embracing you again and telling you with my own lips how well I love you.

Madame de Favras to Marquis de Favras
(1790)

Dear friend, you, the comforter of my pains and woes, you whom I cherish better than my own life, you, who are a thousand times dearer since you have been persecuted, while you are far from deserving it— your loving letter expresses so truly the feelings of your heart for me that I cannot put it out of my sight. I have kissed it, wept over it, pressed it to my heart! You are now far from me; we no longer breathe the same air; I have lost the only consolation I had! It was sweet to me to be near you; far from you, it is death.

Oh, my dear! can you believe that in my eyes there is any stain on your honour—I who know your honesty, your candour?...

I received your vows at the altar with a thrill of happiness which I can never forget. Our hearts, my dear friend, were made for one another; my life is bound up with yours far more by love than by the marriage sacrament.

Lord Nelson to Lady Emma Hamilton
(1803)

All your dear letters *my dear letters*, are so entertaining, and which paint so clearly what you are after, that they give me either the greatest pleasure or pain: it is the next best thing to being with you. I only desire, my dearest Emma, that you will always believe that Nelson's your own, Nelson's Alpha and Omega is Emma, I cannot alter my affection, and love is beyond even this world. Nothing can shake it but yourself, and that I will not allow myself to think for a moment is possible.

I feel that you are the real friend of my bosom, and dearer to me than life, and that I am the same to you; but I will have neither P's or Q's come near you; no, not the slice of single Gloster. But if I was to go on it would argue that want of confidence which would be injurious to your honour. I rejoice that you have had so pleasant a trip to Norfolk, and I hope one day to carry you there by a nearer *tie* in law, but not in more love and affection than at present.

Leigh Hunt to His Betrothed, Marienne (1806)

Dearest Girl,

My journey to Doncaster is deferred till next week, so I sit down to write you a day earlier than I intended, in order that you may have two letters instead of one this week to make up for former deficiencies. A very heavy rain last night has made the snow vanish from the fields, which look delightfully green this morning. I walked out to enjoy the lively air and the universal sunshine, and seated myself with a book on the gateway at the bottom of a little eminence covered with evergreens, a little way from Gainsborough. It seemed the return of spring; a flock of sheep were grazing before me, and cast up every now and then their inquiring visages as much as to say, "What singular being is that so intent upon the mysterious thin substance he is turning over with his hand?" The crows at intervals came wheeling with long cawings above my head; the herds lowed from the surrounding farms; the windmills whirled to the breeze, flinging their huge and rapid shadows on the fields;

and the river Trent sparkled in the sun from east to west. A delightful serenity diffused itself through my heart. I worshipped the magnificence and the love of the God of nature, and I thought of *you*. These two sensations always arise in my heart in the quiet of a rural landscape, and I have often considered it a proof of the purity and the reality of my affection for you, that it always feels most powerful in my religious moments. And this is very natural. Are you not the greatest blessing Heaven has bestowed upon me? Your image attends my rural rambles not only in the healthful walks when, escaped from the clamour of streets and the glare of theatres, I am ready to exclaim with Cowper, "God made the country, and man made the town." It is present with me even in the bustle of life; it gives me a distaste to a frivolous and riotous society; it excites me to improve myself in order to deserve your affection, and it quenches the little flashes of caprice and impatience which disturb the repose of existence. If I feel my anger rising at trifles it checks me instantaneously; it seems to say to me, "Why do you disturb yourself? Marienne loves you; you deserve her love, and ought to be above these little marks of a little mind." Such is the power of love. I am naturally a man of violent passions, but your affection has taught me to subdue them. Whenever you feel any little inquietudes or impatiences arising in your bosom, think of the happiness you bestow upon me, and real love will produce the same effect on you that it produces on me. *No reasoning person ought to marry, who cannot say, "My love has made, me better, and more desirous of improvement than I was before."*

Victor Hugo to Adèle Foucher
(1822)

My dearest Adèle, the first time I see you I want to throw myself at your knees, and kiss the ground under your feet. If you only knew what happiness your letters give me, with what courage they fill me, you would spend all your time in writing to me when you are not with me. As for myself, I let my pen follow the dictates of my heart. My pen runs on, but suddenly I find that I have not words to express what I feel. The very thought of you causes me to feel the inexpressible. You fill my soul as if I were possessed of a divine spirit. I feel at times like worshipping you as the heathen worship their idols. All that is tender, noble, and generous you evoke in me. I respect, venerate, esteem, admire, and love you to the point of adoration. When you tell me to repeat often that I am your husband, you cannot conceive the greatness of my joy.

Yes, I am your husband, your defender, protector, slave. On the day that I lose that conviction I shall have ceased to live, because my life will have lost its foundation. You are the only person to whom I can confide the desire, hope, and love that is within me—my soul itself.

If you want to refrain from distressing me repeat your belief that the proofs of your tenderness and devotion which you deign to give me can call forth nothing but the most respectful and deepest gratitude.

If you only knew how happy I am when I find that she to whom I have confided my happiness confides hers to me! When you unfearingly allow me to enfold your pure virgin form in my arms, then it seems as though you could give me no higher proof of your esteem—yet how fathom the exultation that is aroused by the esteem of an angel!

And so your husband would hope that you will not be inexorable, and that if you love him you will not refuse him a few mornings, like that of the day before yesterday. This I beg of you with all my heart.

Helmuth von Moltke to Mary Burt
(1842)

You write me that you are often depressed, and then again in high spirits. To tell the truth, that is by no means such a good thing as a calmly equable, cheerful disposition; but everyone is so in early youth, and I hope to see you *sweet-tempered* too. Cheerful equanimity is not only a great happiness, but also, in so far as it depends upon ourselves, a duty and a merit. Let us strive after it on both sides, and have no moods, sulks, or pettishness, or, if they do occur, let us see who is ready first to stretch out the hand of reconciliation. Someone has said that there are only two kinds of marriages—those in which the husband is under petticoat rule, and unhappy ones. I desire nothing better than to be at your mercy, and it will be your part to bring me to that point by your gentleness, compliance, and kindness.

Nathaniel Hawthorne to His Wife, Sophia
(1848)

Dearest, I long for thee as thou dost for me. My love has increased infinitely since the last time we were separated. I can hardly bear to think of thy staying away yet weeks longer. I think of thee all the time. The other night, I dreamed that I was at Newton, in a room with thee, and with several other people; and thou tookst occasion to announce, that thou hadst now ceased to be my wife, and hadst taken another husband. Thou madest this intelligence known with such perfect composure and *sang froid*—not particularly addressing me, but the company generally—

that it benumbed my thoughts and feelings, so that I had nothing to say. Thou wast perfectly decided, and I had only to submit without a word. But, hereupon, thy sister Elizabeth, who was likewise present, informed the company, that, in this state of affairs, having ceased to be thy husband, I of course became hers; and turning to me, very coolly inquired whether she or I should write to inform my mother of the new arrangement! How the children were to be divided, I know not. I only know that my heart suddenly broke loose, and I began to expostulate with thee in an infinite agony, in the midst of which I awoke; but the sense of unspeakable injury and outrage hung about me for a long time—and even yet it has not quite departed. Thou shouldst not behave so, when thou comest to me in dreams. . . .

Oh, Phoebe, I want thee much. My bosom needs thy head upon it,— thou alone art essential. Thou art the only person in the world that ever was necessary to me. Other people have occasionally been more or less agreeable; but I think I was always more at ease alone than in anybody's company, till I knew thee. And now I am only myself when thou art within my reach. Thou art an unspeakably beloved woman. How couldst thou inflict such frozen agony upon me, in that dream! Thou shouldst have caressed me and embraced me. . . .

Ownest, if I write any more, it would be only to try to express more lovings, and longings—and as they are impossible to express, I may as well close.

My only belovedest,

THY BEST BELOVED

Mark Twain (Samuel Langhorne Clemens)
to His Wife, Livy
(1875)

Livy Darling,

Six years have gone by since I made my first great success in life and won you, and thirty years have passed since Providence made preparation for that happy success by sending you into the world. Every day we live together adds to the security of my confidence that we can never any more wish to be separated than we can imagine a regret that we were ever joined. You are dearer to me to-day, my child, than you were upon the last anniversary of this birthday; you were dearer then than you were a year before—you have grown more and more dear from the first of those anniversaries, and I do not doubt that this precious progression will continue on to the end—that is, if my strong but sluggishly demonstrative love has not already reached its limit and perfection.

Let us look forward to the coming anniversaries, with their age and their gray hairs, without fear and without depression, trusting and believing that the love we bear each other will be sufficient to make them blessed.

LOVING
COUPLES

Heloïse to Abelard
(ca. 1132?)

Heaven knows! in all my love it was you, and you only, I sought for. I looked for no dowry, no splendid alliances—I was even indifferent to my own pleasures; nor had I a will to gratify. Everything was absorbed in you. . . . The more I humbled myself before you, the greater right, I thought, I should have to your favor; and thus, also, I hoped the less to injure the splendid reputation you had acquired.

The woman who prefers a rich to a poor man shows she has a venal soul. In a husband, it is his wealth, and not himself she admires; and to her who marries with this view some reward may be due, but no gratitude. It is clear that I do not misconstrue her intentions; for propose but a richer match, and, if not too late, she will embrace it with ardor. The truth of my opinion the learned Aspasia has confirmed in a conversation with Xenophon and his wife, as related by Eschines, the disciple of Socrates. When to effect a reconciliation between them she had proposed this reasoning, Aspasia thus concludes: "When you have got so far as mutually to be convinced that there lives not a better man and a more fortunate woman, all your thoughts will be directed to produce the greatest good; Xenophon will be happy in the reflection that he is married to the best of women, and she, on her side, that her husband is the best of men."

These sentiments are beautiful; they seem the production rather of Wisdom herself than of Philosophy. But in the married state, should this favorable opinion be even grounded on error, how charming is it to be thus deceived! It produces love, and on this rests the surest pledge of mutual fidelity; while purity of mind co-operates far more efficaciously than her sister virtue.

But that happiness which in others is sometimes the effect of fancy, in me was the child of evidence. They might think their husbands perfect, and were happy in the idea; but I knew you were such, and the universe knew the same. Thus the more my affection was secured from all possible error, the more steady became its flame. Where was found the king or the philosopher that had emulated your reputation? Was there a village, a city, a kingdom, that did not ardently wish to see you? When you appeared in public, who did not run to behold you? And when you withdrew, every neck was stretched, every eye sprang forward to follow you. The women, married, and unmarried, when Abelard was away, longed for his return: and when he was present, every bosom was on fire. No lady of distinction, no princess, even, that did not envy Heloïse the possession of her Abelard.

Abelard to Heloïse
(ca. 1132?)

When formerly I was with you, you recollect, my dear Heloïse, how fervently you recommended me to the care of Providence. Often in the day a special prayer was offered up for me. Removed as I am now from the Paraclete, and involved in great danger, how much more pressing are my wants! Now then convince me of the sincerity of your regard. I entreat, I implore you.

But if, by the will of heaven, my enemies should so far prevail as to take away my life; or if by any chance I should be numbered with the dead, it is my prayer that my body be conveyed to the Paraclete. There my daughters, or rather my sisters in Christ, turning their eyes often to my tomb, will more strongly be excited to petition heaven for me. And indeed, to a mind penetrated with grief, and stricken by the dark view of its crimes, where can be found a resting-place, at once so safe, and so full of hope, as that which in a peculiar manner is dedicated to, and bears the name of Paraclete, which is, the Comforter? Besides I know not where a Christian could find a better grave than in the society of holy women, consecrated to God. They, as the Gospel tells us, attended the interment of their divine master; they embalmed his body with precious perfumes, they followed him to the sepulchre, and there they watched in anxious solicitude. In return they were consoled with the first angelic apparition, announcing his resurrection, and many subsequent favors were conferred upon them. To conclude, it is my most earnest request that the solicitude you now so strongly feel for the preservation of my life, you will then extend to the repose of my soul. Carry into my grave the same degree of love you showed me when alive, that is, never forget to petition heaven for me in your prayers. Heloïse, live, and farewell! Farewell, my sisters; live, but let it be in Christ! Remember Abelard!

Heloïse to Abelard
(ca. 1132?)

You request, should your death happen while absent from us, that your body be conveyed to the Paraclete; for thus you think, with your image ever before us, to derive greater benefit from our prayers. Do you then imagine we can ever forget you? Or will that be a season for prayer, when general consternation shall have banished every tranquil thought; when reason will have lost its sway, and the tongue its utterance; when the mind, in frantic rage, rebelling against its maker, will not seek to pacify him by supplications, but rather to provoke his angel by complaints? On that sad day our sole occupation will be to weep, but not to pray. We shall follow you; we shall step into the tomb with you. How then are we to perform the last melancholy rites? With you having lost the support of our lives, what will remain for us but death? God grant that day may be our last! If the mere mention of your death thus strikes us to the heart, what will not the reality do? It is our prayer to heaven that we may not survive you, that we may never have to perform that office which we expect from your hands.

Again let us entreat you to be more considerate for the sake of us all; at least, on my account do refrain from all expressions which, like the shafts of death, penetrate my soul. The mind, worn down by grief, is a stranger to repose; plunged in troubles, it is little able to think on God. To him you have devoted our lives; and will you impede his service? It were to be wished that every necessary event which brings sorrow with it, might take place when least expected; for what cannot be avoided by human foresight, when permitted to torment us, only raises unavailing fears. But if I lose you, what have I to hope for? You are my only comfort; deprived of that, shall I still drag on my miserable pilgrimage? But even in you, what comfort have I, save only the thought that you are still living? All other joys are forbidden to me. I may not be allowed to see you, that my soul might sometimes, at least, return into its own bosom.

May I be permitted to say that heaven has never ceased to be my relentless persecutor? If you call it clemency, where is cruelty to be found? Fortune, that savage destiny, has spent against me every arrow of her rage. She has none left to throw at others. Her quiver was full, and she exhausted it on me. Mortals have no longer cause to dread her. Nor if there were a shaft left would it find in Heloïse a spot to light on. But though bleeding at every pore, my enemy does not stay her persecuting hand; she suspends the last fatal stroke, and only fears lest my wounds prove mortal. Of all the wretched, I am the most forlorn and wretched! Preferred by you to the rest of my sex, I rose to the most exalted dignity: thrown down from thence, my fate has been proportionately hard. He who falls from the greatest height falls with the greatest risk. Where was the woman of birth or power that fortune would have dared to compare with me? In the possession of you my glory was unrivalled; so is my disgrace in your privation. In prosperity and in adversity my life has known no measure. My happiness was unbounded, so is my affliction. Pondering over my melancholy state, I shed the more tears when I consider the magnitude of my losses; but my tears redouble when I remember how dear those pleasures were which I have lost. To the greatest joys have succeeded the greatest sorrows.

Abelard to Heloïse
(ca. 1132?)

You have professed a willingness to follow me even to the gates of misery, and will you let me go without you to those of eternal happiness? Let this, at least, be a motive which may urge you to a religious life. Reflect on the happiness which awaits you there, and on my society, which will no more be taken from you, for you do not hesitate to declare that I am in the right way. Recollect what you once said; call to mind the words of your last letter, that in the manner of our conversion, and in the mode of God's chastisement, heaven had been rather favorable to me. Yes, Heloïse, it was kind to us both; but the excess of your grief does not admit the language of reason. Lament not that you were the cause of this event; rather be persuaded you were born to be it. I suffered; but it was advantageous to me; do the sufferings of the martyrs also give you pain? Had I justly suffered, could you have borne it more patiently? If so, ignominy would have fallen upon me, and my enemies might have gloried; they would have been just, and I contemptible. Their conduct would have found no accusers, and who would have pitied me?

To assuage the bitterness of your grief I could show that all has happened for the best, and with a view to our greater good. The ways of Providence are inscrutable but just. Revolve in your thoughts the intemperance of our behavior, even after marriage, when you were at

Argenteuil, and I sometimes came to visit you. Need I mention our many antecedent caresses? and how basely I had deceived your uncle, when I lived with him in habits of unlimited confidence? Surely his vengeance was not unmerited. It was in punishment of these crimes that I have suffered; and to the same cause I ascribe the many evils which, at this hour, surround me. It will be well if divine justice may thus be satisfied. Call to your recollection another circumstance. When I took you from Paris into Brittany, to avoid shame and the fury of your uncle, you disguised yourself in the habit of a nun, and thus irreverently profaned the holy institute you now profess. With what propriety, then has the divine justice, or rather, the divine goodness, compelled you to embrace a state which you could wantonly ridicule, willing that in the very habit of a nun you should expiate the crime committed against it. The truth of reality supplies itself a cure, and corrects your dissimulation.

If we view the advantages also which this justice has produced, you will rather be disposed to bless the kindness of heaven towards us. My dearest Heloïse, do consider, from what perils we were drawn, even when we resisted most the calls of mercy. We were exposed to the most dangerous tempests, and God delivered us. Ever repeat, and with a grateful mind, the wonders of His mercy. The worst sinners may take a lesson from our example; for what may not suppliants expect, when they hear of the favors which were done to us? Compare together the magnitude of our dangers, and the ease of our deliverance; our inveterate disorders, and the gentle remedy: our unworthy conduct, and the benevolence of heaven. I will then proclaim what the Lord has done for me.

And do you also be my inseparable associate in this grateful thanksgiving: you were my partner in guilt, and you shared the favor of heaven.

Henry VIII to Anne Boleyn
(1528)

~~~∞~~~

The approach of the time for which I have so long waited rejoices me so much, that it seems almost to have come already. However, the entire accomplishment cannot be till the two persons meet, which meeting is more desired by me than anything in this world; for what joy can be greater upon earth than to have the company of her who is dearest to me, knowing likewise that she does the same on her part, the thought of which gives me the greatest pleasure.

Judge what an effect the presence of that person must have on me, whose absence has grieved my heart more than either words or writing can express and which nothing can cure, but that begging you, my mistress, to tell your father from me, that I desire him to hasten the day appointed by two days, that he may be at court before the old term, or at farthest on the day prefixed, for otherwise I shall think he will not do the lover's turn, as he said he would, nor answer my expectation.

No more at present for lack of time, hoping shortly that by word of mouth I shall tell you the rest of the sufferings endured by me from your absence.

Written by the hand of the secretary, who wishes himself at this moment privately with you, and who is, and always will be,

Your loyal and most assured servant,

H. NO OTHER (A. B.) SEEKS, R.

Anne Boleyn to Henry VIII
(ca. 1530?)

Sir,

It belongs only to the august mind of a great king, to whom Nature has given a heart full of generosity towards the sex, to repay by favours so extraordinary, an artless and short conversation with a girl. Inexhaustible as is the treasury of your majesty's bounties, I pray you to consider that it cannot be sufficient to your generosity; for if you recompense so slight a conversation by gifts so great, what will you be able to do for those who are ready to consecrate their entire obedience to your desires? How great soever may be the bounties I have received, the joy I feel in being loved by a king whom I adore, and to whom I would with pleasure make a sacrifice of my heart, if fortune had rendered it worthy of being offered to him, will ever be infinitely greater.

The warrant of maid of honour to the Queen induces me to think that your majesty has some regard for me. Since it gives me the means of seeing you oftener, and of assuring you by my own lips (which I shall do on the first opportunity) that I am,

Your majesty's very obliged and very obedient servant, without any reserve,

ANNE BOLEYN

Margaret of Valois to James, Lord of Chanvallon
(ca.1580?)

Certain it is, dear heart, that love is a sophist and full of persuasions, since it furnishes you with so many arguments as almost to put truth in doubt. I have not decided, however, to surrender, believing that there is more glory in conquering where there is more resistance. I know that you would say what you have often said, having learned it of me, that it is easier to brave an absent enemy; and surely I admit that, as I do that your presence might render natural things,—which is love itself.

But what gives me strength is the fact that I know how to preserve your opinion, since the same natural law governs all our actions. Your soul wishes what I wish, and I am glad to please it. Soul and the physical in man are the two elements which are sufficient to respond to every desire, longing, or appetite, and all these are concentrated in the desire for beauty,—beauty in spiritual, and beauty in natural things,—which is love itself.

There are two kinds of love: love of the soul and love of the body. The former consists of the intercourse of virtues, and the latter of lines and colours. The first is only understood by the mind, aided by the heart; the second by the eyes, there being no other thing in us which can judge it. Now, if unworthy cravings or desires take possession of this twofold love, all thought of beauty is banished. Look to the difference, and be not deceived by the similar terms of things so unlike in nature, and know you that, whether you be philosopher or lover, you must acknowledge my logic, which finds in you so perfectly the true subject of true love, which causes me to pledge my eternal and complete troth.

Thus full of this divine and far from vulgar passion, I waft in my imagination a thousand kisses to your beautiful mouth, which alone shall be the participant in the pleasure reserved for the soul, meriting it because it is the instrument of so many beautiful and worthy compliments, which have quite seduced me.

Farewell, my life, my king, my all.

James, Lord of Chanvallon, to Margaret of Valois (ca.1580?)

I did not dare to disturb you while you were so plunged in your devotions; but today, my Queen, I hope that you will be able to begin to send, as one would say, God into Galilee, for I fear not to return to the errors of my ways while you have the power, not only to keep me from them, but to crown my greatest felicity with your perfections.

I had promised myself that I should have the honour of seeing you yesterday: I beg you very humbly that it may be this evening, and that you will say that I have discovered to you an infinity of things which I have learned, it matters not where. I do not think that you should know of the past when that past has taught me something; but you will permit me, dear heart, to see you this evening, and to speak with you; and do not excuse yourself, at your peril, the which I am nevertheless convinced will not prevent you from doing what you please—and so let us hope that the world will betake itself to bed earlier than is its wont, and slumber more deeply. Farewell, my beautiful mistress. I kiss your fair hands most humbly.

John Winthrop to Margaret Tyndal
(1618)

To my best beloved, Mrs. Margaret Tyndal, at
Great Maplestead, Essex. Grace, mercy, and peace, &c.

My own beloved spouse, my most sweet friend and faithful companion of my pilgrimage, the happy and hopeful supply (next Christ Jesus) of my greatest losses, I wish thee a most plentiful increase of all true comfort in the love of Christ, with a large and prosperous addition of whatsoever happiness the sweet estate of holy wedlock, in the kindest society of a loving husband, may afford thee. Being filled with the joy of thy love, and wanting opportunity of more familiar communion with thee, which my heart fervently desires, I am constrained to ease the burthen of my mind by this poor help of my scribbling pen, being sufficiently assured that, although my presence is that which thou desirest, yet in the want thereof these lines shall not be unfruitful of comfort unto thee. And now, my sweet love, let me awhile solace myself in the remembrance of our love, of which this springtime of our acquaintance can put forth as yet no more but the leaves and blossoms, whilst the fruit lies wrapped up in the tender bud of hope; a little more patience will disclose this good fruit, and bring it to some maturity. Let it be our care and labour to preserve these hopeful buds from the beasts of the field, and from frosts and other injuries of the air, lest our fruit fall off ere it be ripe, or lose aught in the beauty and pleasantness of it. Let us pluck up such nettles and thorns as would defraud our plants of their due nourishment; let us prune off superfluous branches; let us not stick at some labour in watering and manuring them: the plenty and goodness of our fruit shall recompense us abundantly. Our trees are planted in a fruitful soil; the ground and pattern of our love is no other but that between Christ and his dear spouse, of whom she speaks as she finds him. "My well-beloved is mine and I am his." Love was their banqueting-house, love was their wine, love was their ensign; love was his invitings, love was her faintings; love was his apples, love was her comforts; love was his embracings, love was her refreshing; love made him see her, love made her seek him; love made him wed her, love made her follow him; love made him her saviour, love made her his servant. Love bred our fellowship, let love continue it, and love shall increase it until death dissolve it. . . .

Lastly, for my farewell (for thou seest my lothness to part with thee makes me tedious), take courage unto thee, and cheer up thy heart in the Lord, for thou knowest that Christ, the best of husbands, can never fail thee: he never dies, so as there can be no grief at parting; he never changes, so as once beloved and ever the same; his ability is ever infinite, so as the dowry and inheritance of his sons and daughters can never be diminished. As for me, a poor worm, dust and ashes, a man full of infirmities, subject to all sins, changes, and chances which befall the sons of men, how should I promise thee anything of myself, or, if I should, what credence couldst thou give thereto, seeing God only is true and every man a liar? Yet so far as a man may presume upon some experience, I may tell thee that my hope is, that such comfort as thou hast already conceived of my love towards thee shall (through God's blessing) be happily continued; his grace shall be sufficient for me, and his power shall be made perfect in my greatest weakness; only let thy godly, kind, and sweet carriage towards me be as fuel to the fire, to minister a constant supply of meet matter to the confirming and quickening of my dull affections. This is one end why I write so much unto thee, that if there should be any decay in kindness, &c., through my default and slackness hereafter, thou might have some patterns of our first love by thee, to help the recovery of such disease. Yet let our trust be wholly in God, and let us constantly follow him by our prayers, complaining and moaning unto him of our poverty, imperfections, and unworthiness, until his fatherly affection break forth upon us, and he speak kindly to the hearts of his poor servant and handmaid, for the full assurance of grace and peace through Christ Jesus, to whom I now leave thee (my sweet spouse and only beloved). God send us a safe and comfortable meeting on Monday morning. Farewell. Remember my love and duty to my Lady, thy good mother, with all kind and due salutations to thy uncle E. and all thy brothers and sisters.

Thy husband by promise,

JOHN WINTHROP

Margaret Winthrop (née Margaret Tyndal) to John Winthrop (1627)

My most sweet Husband,

How dearly welcome thy kind letter was to me I am not able to express. The sweetness of it did much refresh me. What can be more pleasing to a wife than to hear of the welfare of her best beloved, and how he is pleased with her poor endeavours? I blush to hear myself commended, knowing my own wants. But it is your love that conceives the best, and makes all things seem better than they are. I wish that I may always be pleasing to thee, and that those comforts we have in each other may be daily increased, as far as they be pleasing to God. I will use that speech to thee that Abigail did to David; I will be a servant to wash the feet of my lord. I will do any service wherein I may please my good husband. I confess I cannot do enough for thee: but thou art pleased to accept the will for the deed, and rest contented.

I have many reasons to make me love thee, whereof I will name two: first, because thou lovest God; and secondly, because thou lovest me. If these two were wanting, all the rest would be eclipsed. But I must leave this discourse, and go about my household affairs. I am a bad housewife to be so long from them; but I must needs borrow a little time to talk with thee, my sweet heart. The term is more than half done. I hope thy business draws to an end. It will be but two or three weeks before I see thee, though they be long ones. God will bring us together in his good time; for which I shall pray. I thank the Lord we are all in good health. We are very glad to hear so good news of our son Henry. The Lord make us thankful for all his mercies to us and ours. And thus, with my mother's and my own best love to yourself and all the rest, I shall leave this scribbling. The weather being cold makes me make haste. Farewell, my good husband; the Lord keep thee.

Your obedient wife,

Margaret Winthrop

Charles I to Henrietta Maria
(1643)

Dear Heart,

I never knew till now the good of ignorance; for I did not know the danger that thou wert in by the storm before I had assurance of thy happy escape, we having had a pleasing false report of thy safe landing at Newcastle, which thine of the 19th January so confirmed us in, that we at least were not undeceived of that hope until we knew certainly how great a danger thou hadst passed, of which I shall not be out of apprehension until I may have the happiness of thy company. For indeed I think it not the least of my misfortunes, that for my sake thou hast run so much hazard; in which thou hast expressed so much love to me, that I confess it is impossible to repay by anything I can do, much less by words. But my heart being full of affection of thee, admiration of thee, and impatient passion of gratitude to thee, I could not but say something, leaving the rest to be read by thee out of thine own noble heart.

CHARLES R.

Henrietta Maria to Charles I
(1643)

My Dear Heart,

I received your letters, the last of which puts me in no small pain for having hurt you so much; but I hope you will believe that it was the care I have for you, and my affection, which made me act as I did; for I protest to you that it is for your sake alone that I am angry or displeased; for, as to my private self, I would rather live out of the world than suffer all that I have suffered in it, and I have sufficient knowledge that no one can be happy, even in prosperity, in it, to retire from it; for it is but deceit. I have had enough of it to have experienced what both are, and can be a good judge, and both show me too well the contempt in which it should be held. This is not written in anger, but comes from a mind very resolute, and not frightened by our affairs; for had I to suffer a thousand times more than I have done, which is I think impossible enough, I should not be rebuffed; on the contrary, I should strengthen myself against misfortunes. But if you were as you should be, you would see that all my actions and thoughts have been but for you, and that it was only my affections which made me do all that I have done, or written. Therefore, if that be any fault, let me confess it; since you think it, I recognise and confess it, and hope for absolution; and

I know well that when I speak to you, you will say I have been more in the right to write as I did than you now think, though I confess I was wrong in something.

Adieu, my dear heart.

Count Königsmarck to Sophia Dorothea
(1692)

I imagined that in possessing your love I should be the happiest man in the world. I little thought I should have so few opportunities of speaking to you. I tell you frankly this continual restraint falls far short of perfect felicity, and my happiness will never be complete until I enter upon it wholly. Believe me, this is true. I was speaking to La Confidente about it last night; she will tell you my wishes. I have to talk to you just like everyone else, and precautions have to be taken, though they wound and vex us. Let us hope for better times, for until then we are doomed to suffer. Meanwhile forget nothing that will give me comfort, and assure me of your tender love; you cannot do this better than in letting me see you as often as possible. Did you really notice how the Duchess of Saxe-Eisenach attacked me? I hope when I have answered her two or three times as curtly as possible, she will clearly understand that I want no intercourse with her.

Your kind note assures me of your tender love; and assurances must suffice for the present. But I am not the man to let myself be made sport of, and if your promises do not agree with your conduct they will not make the slightest impression on me. You have not treated me very well the last two days, and I cannot quite believe your notes; but if you change your manner, I am quite ready to accept your protestations. I am forced to assume an extremely distant manner towards you, and it makes me furious; I wish you could alter it, but you cannot. Pardon me once more. It is my hot temper—I know it, but you are the cause.

Sophia Dorothea to Count Königsmarck
(1692)

I spent the hours of the night without sleeping, and all the day thinking of you, weeping over our separation. Never did a day seem so long to me; I do not know how I shall ever get reconciled to your absence. La Gouvernante has just given me your letter; I received it with rapture. Rest assured I will do even more than I have promised, and lose no opportunity of showing you my love. If I could shut myself up while you are away, and see no one, I would do so gladly, for without you everything is distasteful and wearisome. Nothing can make your absence bearable to me; I am faint with weeping. I hope to prove by my life that no woman has ever loved man as I love you, and no faithfulness will ever equal mine. In spite of every trial and all that may befall, nothing will sever me from you. Of a truth, dear one, my love will only end with my life.

I was so changed and depressed today that even the Prince, my husband, pitied me, and said I was ill and ought to take care of myself. He is right—I am ill; but my illness comes only from loving you, and I never wish to be cured. I have not seen anyone worth mentioning. I went to visit the Duchess [of Celle], but returned home as soon as possible, to have the joy of talking about you with La Confidente. La Gazelle's husband came to wish me goodbye; I saw him in my room, and he kissed my hand.

It is now eight o'clock, and I must go and pay my court. How dull I shall seem—how stupid! I shall withdraw immediately after supper, so that I may have the pleasure of reading your letters again, the only pleasure I have while you are away. Farewell, my worshipped one. Only death will sever me from you; all human powers will never succeed. Remember all your promises, and be as constant as I shall be faithful.

Hester Vanhomrigh to Jonathan Swift
(ca. 1714?)

Is it possible that you will do the very same thing I warned you of so lately? I believe you thought I only rallied you when I told you the other night that I would pester you with letters. Did not I know you very well I should think you knew but little of the world, to imagine that a woman would not keep her word whenever she promised anything so malicious. Had not you better a thousand times throw away one hour at some time or other of the day than be interrupted in your business at this rate; for I know 't is as impossible for you to burn my letters without reading them as 'tis for me to avoid reproving you when you behave yourself wrong. Once more I advise you, if you have any regard for your own quiet, to alter your behaviour quickly, for I do assure you I have too much spirit to sit down contented with this treatment. Because I love darkness extremely, I here tell you now that I have determined to try all manner of human arts to reclaim you, and if all these fail, I am resolved to have recourse to the black art, which, it is said, never does. Now see what inconveniences you will bring both me and yourself into. Pray think calmly of it. Is it not better to come of yourself than to be brought by force, and that perhaps at a time when you have the most agreeable engagement in the world? for when I undertake to do anything I don't propose to do it by halves. But there is one thing falls out very luckily for you, which is, that of all the passions, revenge hurries me least, so that you have it yet in your power to turn all this fury into good humour, and depend on it, and more, I assure you. Come at what time you please you can never fail of being very well received.

Jonathan Swift to Hester Vanhomrigh
(ca. 1714?)

If you write as you do, I shall come the seldomer on purpose to be pleased with your letters, which I never look into without wondering how a brat who cannot read can possibly write so well. You are mistaken. Send me a letter without your hand on the outside and I hold you a crown I shall not read it. But, raillery apart, I think it inconvenient, for a hundred reasons, that I should make your house a sort of constant dwelling-place. I will certainly come as often as I conveniently can; but health and the perpetual run of ill-weather hinders me from going out in the morning, and my afternoons are so taken up, I know now how, that I am in rebellion with a dozen people beside yourself for not seeing them. For the rest you need make use of no black art besides your wits. 'Tis a pity your eyes are not black, or I should have said the same of them; but you are a white witch and can do no mischief. If you have employed any of your arts on the black scarf I defy it for one reason. Guess. Adieu, for Dr. P——'s come in to see me.

Lord Peterborough to Henrietta Howard
(ca. 1722?)

Change of air, the common remedy, has no effect; and flight, the refuge of all who fear, gives me no manner of security or ease; a fair devil haunts me wherever I go, though perhaps not so malicious as the black ones, yet more tormenting. How much more tormenting is the beauteous devil than the ugly one! The first I am always thinking of, the other seldom comes in my thoughts; the terrors of the ugly devil very often diminish upon consideration, but the oppressions of the fair one become more intolerable every time she comes into my mind. The chief attribute of the devil is tormenting. Who could look upon you, and give you that title? Who can feel what I do, and give you any other?

But most certainly I have more to lay to the charge of the fair one than can be objected to Satan or Beelzebub. We may believe that they only have a mind to torment because they are tormented; if they endeavour to procure us misery it is because they are in pain; they must be our companions in suffering, but my white devil partakes none of my torments.

In a word, give me Heaven, for it is in your power, or you may have an equal hell! Judge of the disease by the extravagant symptoms; one moment I curse you, the next I pray for you. Oh, hear my prayers or I am miserable! Forgive me if I threaten you; take this for a proof as well as punishment. If you can prove inhuman you shall have reproaches from Moscow, China, or the barbarous quarters of Tartary.

Believe me, for I think I am in earnest. This I am sure of: I could not endure my ungrateful country but for your sake.

Henrietta Howard to Lord Peterborough
(ca. 1722?)

I have carefully perused your Lordship's letter about your fair devil and your black devil, your hell and tortures, your Heaven and happiness—those sublime expressions which ladies and gentlemen use in their gallantries and distresses.

I suppose by your fair devil you mean nothing less than an angel. If so, my Lord, I beg leave to give some reasons why I think a woman is neither like an angel nor a devil, and why successful and unhappy love do not in the least resemble Heaven and hell. It is true, you may quote these thousand gallant letters and precedents for the use of these love terms, which have a mighty captivating sound in the ears of a woman, and have been with equal propriety applied to all women in all ages.

In the first place, my Lord, an angel pretends to be nothing else but a *spirit.* If, then, a woman was no more than an angel, what could a lover get by the pursuit? The black devil is a spirit too, but one that has lost her beauty and retained her pride. Tell a woman this, and ask how she likes the simile. The pleasure of an angel is offering praise; the pleasure of a woman is receiving it.

Successful love is very unlike Heaven, because you may have success one hour, and lose it the next. Heaven is unchangeable. Who can say so of love and letters? In love there are as many Heavens as there are women; so that, if a man be so unhappy as to lose one Heaven, he need not throw himself headlong into hell.

This thought might be carried further. But perhaps you will ask me if a woman be neither like angel or devil, what is she like ? I answer that the only thing that is like a woman is—*another woman.*

How often has your Lordship persuaded foreign ladies that nothing but them could make you forsake your dear country. But at present I find it is more to your purpose to tell me that I am the only woman that could prevail with you to stay in your ungrateful country.

Lord Peterborough to Henrietta Howard
(ca. 1722?)

Love is the general word, but upon many occasions very improperly used; for passions very different, if not quite opposite, go under the same title.

I have found love in so many disguises and false appearances in others, and even in myself, that I thought the true passion undiscoverable and impossible to be described; but what I pretend to represent I have so frequently felt, that methinks I should be the better able to express it.

The beginnings of this passion, whether true or false, are pleasing; but if true, the progress is through mountains and rocks. The unhappy traveller goes through rugged ways, and, what is most cruel, he is walking in the dark on the edge of precipices; he labours under a thousand difficulties;—success must cost him dear, and then, alas! the acquisition is insecure.

The greatest hardship is this: we seem bound to the same port, we sail in treacherous seas in quest of a woman's heart, but without a compass; there is no beaten path or common road; as many objects, so many humours; what prevails with one may displease the other in this fantastic pilgrimage of love; he that goes out of his way may soonest arrive at his journey's end; and the bold have better success than the faithful, the foolish than the wise.

But I have undertaken to define this passion which I allow to be called *love*. It is not the person who could please me most, but her that I am most desirous to please, who is truly adored.

To judge of this let us consider the character of a beauteous female coquette. This creature seems designed to give a man pleasure, and pleasure without pain, though not qualified to give him love; access is easy, enjoyment sure. Free from restraint or obligations, not fettered with the chains of pretended constancy, you meet her with satisfaction and you part with ease; and are warm enough for pleasure, not exposed to the heats of jealousy, and safe from the cold of despair. A true epicure (but not a lover) can content himself with this, and this may be agreed to be the pleasure-giving lady.

This is no unlively picture of a woman who can please, but far from that person to whom we resign our hearts in the delicate way of love. How shall I describe the woman capable of inspiring a true, respectful tenderness? Who so fills the soul with herself that she leaves room for no other ideas but those of endeavouring to serve and please her? Self-interest, self-satisfaction, are too natural, too powerful, to be quite destroyed, but they are in a manner laid asleep when at the same time we respect and fear her whom we love.

I must always more or less endeavour to maintain by proof what I assert, but I am not at liberty to pursue a pleasure that may give you too much trouble at a time. I begin my next with telling you what *Amoret* should be, or what I think she is.

Henrietta Howard to Lord Peterborough
(ca. 1722?)

One would imagine, by observing upon the world, that every man thought it necessary to be in love—just as he does to talk—to show his superiority to a brute; but such pretenders have only convinced us that they want that quality they would be thought to have.

How few are there born with souls capable of friendship! then how much fewer must there be capable of love, for love includes friendship and much more besides! That you might mistake love in *others*, I grant you; but I wonder how you could mistake it in *yourself*. I should have thought, if anybody else had said so, he had never been in love.

Those rocks and precipices and those mighty difficulties which you say are to be undergone in the progress of love, can only be meant in the pursuit of a coquette, or where there is no hope of a sincere return. Or perhaps you may suppose all women incapable of being touched with so delicate a passion.

In the voyage of love, you complain of great hardships, narrow seas, and no compass. You still think all women coquettes. He that can use art to subdue a woman is not in love; for how can you suppose a man capable of acting by reason who has not one of his senses under command? Do you think a lover sees or hears his mistress like standers-by? Whatever her looks may be, or however she talks, he sees nothing but roses and lilies, and hears only an angel.

The civilities of some women seem to me, like those of shop-keepers, to encourage a multitude of customers. Who is so obliging to all her lovers as a coquette? She can express her civilities with the utmost ease and free-dom to all her admirers alike; while the person that *loves*, entirely neglects or forgets everybody for the sake of *one*. *To a woman who loves, every man is an impertinent who declares his passion, except the one man she loves.*

Your coquette or "pleasure-giving lady" that can part from you without regret, that cannot feel jealousy, and does not pretend to constancy, I should think a very undesirable thing. I have always imagined that they thought it necessary at least to feign love in order to make themselves agreeable, and that the best dissemblers were the most admired.

Every one that loves thinks his own mistress an Amoret, and therefore ask any lover who and what Amoret is, and he will describe his own mistress as she appears to himself; but the common practice of men of gallantry is to make an Amoret of every lady they write to. And, my lord, after you have summed up all the fine qualities necessary to make an Amoret, I am under some apprehensions you will conclude with a compliment, by saying, *I am she.*

Margaritta Fitzherbert to George IV
(ca. 1784?)

Public calumny I am above; my own reasons and observation are the charms that forbid a private meeting. Already has the notice bestowed on me at the ball by your Royal Highness brought on me the envy of my own sex and the impertinence of yours. I like not your associates, particularly that wild man, H., who stares me out of countenance. The difference of our rank in life forbids a further knowledge of me, and I entreat you to avoid me. I shall be tonight at the ball, not because I like it, but my not having appeared since the last is, I find, observed; and some of our visitors yesterday told me I was too much engaged by the Prince's notice to bestow any on those beneath him. Come to the ball, dance with Lady B., and take the slightest notice of me. Why should you wish to take more? There are a hundred much prettier women!

Mrs. O. for example—you think her pretty. She is indeed divine! And she has a husband, an officer of spirit, to shield her from the rude attacks of envy. You may enjoy her conversation, she yours, and malice dare not speak. But *me*, an unprotected, helpless orphan? It will be cruel to pursue the humble

MARGARITTA

George IV to Margaritta Fitzherbert
(ca. 1784?)

Cold, unkind, Margaritta! Why am I forbid that attention which is your due—which all the world must pay you? Why am I doomed to pass an insipid evening with a woman of fashion *only*, when my heart and my better judgment would lead me to the most elegant, the most accomplished fair that Brighton has to boast. Mrs. O. is beauteous, but it is not mere beauty I admire, it is expression, "a something than beauty dearer." You know my opinion of Lady B.; her rank entitles her to my hand, nothing besides could induce me. I respect her Grace for the sake of the best of mothers, and therefore I comply with what politeness and etiquette requires; but why must I give up the enjoyment of your conversation? Be superior to common talk.

Call not yourself unprotected—all the world must be your friends. I am concerned H. displeases you. I am certain he never designed it. This wild man has really some good points; that he admires you I wonder not, and perhaps he is not perfectly delicate in that admiration. Does S. likewise displease you, and little J. O., that you say you do not like my associates? If they do, they shall not trouble you; I want no company when in yours!

I felt your absence from the ball, and rejoice that you will grace it this evening. It is impossible to see you with indifference! In vain would you exact so hard a task from the tenderest of your friends,

The obliged

WALES

Henry Frederick, Duke of Cumberland
to Lady Grosvenor
(ca. 1769?)

My dear little Angel,

I wrote my last letter to you yesterday at eleven o'clock just when we sailed I dined at two o'clock and as for the afternoon I had some music I have my own servant a-board that plays . . . and so got to bed about 10—I then prayed for you *my dearest love kissed your dearest little hair* and laye down and dreamt of you had you on the dear little *couch* ten thousand times in my arms kissing you and telling you how much I loved and adored you and you seem pleased but alas when I woke it found it all dillusion *nobody by me but myself at sea*. . . . I am sure the account of this days duty can be no pleasure to you my love yet it is exactly what I have done and as I promised you always to let you know my motions and thoughts I have now performed my promise this day to you and always will untill the very last letter you shall have from me. . . .

When I shall return to you that instant O' my love mad and happy beyond myself to tell you how I love you and have thought of you ever since I have been separated from you. . . . I hope you are well I am sure I need not tell you I have had nothing in my thoughts but your dearself and long for the time to come back again to you I will all the while take care of myself because you desire *my dear little Friend* does the angel of my heart pray do you take care of your dearself for the sake of your faithful servant who lives but to love you to adore you, and to bless the moment that has made you generous enough to own it to him I hope my dear nay I will dare to say you never will have reason to repent it. . . .

Indeed my dear angel I need not tell you I know you read the reason too well that made me do so it was to write to you for God knows I wrote to no one else nor shall I at any other but to the King God bless you most amiable and dearest little creature living—

> Aimons toujours mon adorable petite amour je
> Vous adore plusque la vie mesme

I have been reading for about an hour this morning in Prior and find these few lines just now applicable to us—

> How oft had *Henry* changed his sly disguise,
> Unmarked by all but beauteous Harriet's eyes:
> Oft had found means alone to see the dame,
> And at the feet to breathe his am'rous flame:
> And oft the pain of absence to remove
> By letters soft interpreters of love
> Till time and industry (the mighty two
> That bring our wishes nearer to our view)
> Made him perceive that the inclining fair
> Received his vows with no reluctant ear;
> That Venus had confirmed her equal reign
> And dealt to Harriet's heart a share of *Henry's* pain.

Such is my amusement to read those sorts of things that puts me in mind of our mutual feelings and situations now. God bless you till I shall again have an opportunity of sending to you, I shall write to you a letter a day as many days as you miss herein of me when I do they shall all come Friday 16th June God bless I shant forget you God knows you have told me so before I have your heart and it lies warm at my breast I hope mine feels as easy to you thou joy of my life adieu.

Lady Grosvenor to Henry Frederick, Duke of Cumberland (ca. 1790?)

O my dearest Soul I'v just received Two the dearest letters in the World from you, how can I, I cannot express my feelings of gratitude & Love for you, your dear heart is so safe with *me* and feels every motion mine does, with you, how happy your dearest letters make me I'm so much obliged to you for saying you will take care of your dear Health because I desire you, do my dearest Friend I intreat you, & I'll do the same, how sweet those verses are you sent me they are heavenly sweet because they were marked by you I always liked Prior but shall adore him because you like him. I'm made quite happy to night by having fresh assurances of yr love, you have mine intirely how happy will that day be to me that brings you back I wonder where I shall see you first I form a thousand happy ideas to myself I shall be unable to speak from Joy, in the mean time let us write as often as possible.

How kind it was of you to say you had letters of consequence to write when it was only to poor me, Your dear little heart is flurried too on reading ye dear letters it has both laught and cry'd with Joy, it lies warm on my breast I cherish it and think of nothing else but to preserve it safe there and happy.

My dearest Soul I send you Ten Thousand kisses I wish I could give them—

God bless you I will now conclude for I'm sure this letter is stupid enough to tire you to death pray forgive it I'm finishing it in the dark, I see nobody to tell me anything to make my letter entertaining, so can only tell you how sincerely I do and ever shall love you, & I know you'll like that as well as anything for nothing makes me so happy as your telling me so & we love too well not to live by sympathy.

Amons tout Jour Tendrement mon adorable ammi mon tres chere ame.

I'll write again everyday and send it to Reda at all opportunities God bless you *my dearest Dear life I shall ever love you*

Caroline von Linsingen to William IV
(ca. 1791?)

Oh, William, let me then once more part from you thus! The bond by which our hearts are knit can ne'er be rent; yet in this world we are for ever parted. These last three years—perhaps they are not altogether the most terrible of my life, for I could hourly be with you in thought; I could long for death, and could seek it. Now all is changed; duty calls me, and I must, I will do her bidding. Dark and dreary seems to me my future path; nameless is the pain with which I part from you; but I must rely upon my own strength, and no note of anguish shall deter me. Beloved husband,—I may once more call you that,—realise how Caroline loves you, feel it by what she thus sacrifices for you, and ask yourself whence she could have got this power, if love had not given it to her. Spirituality and love can alone— But in an hour the messenger is to start—in one hour! Oh, William, now indeed can I feel the terror of the sinner on the day of judgment! Now I know what it is to die, for now, now only, am I actually to part from you!

With burning, quivering lips have I just kissed your picture, the picture which you used so often in those blissful hours to rob of its kisses, when I grew playfully wrath with the original. God! in what thoughts do I lose myself!

There is yet one thing that I would say to you before I end. I know it, and with the greatest certainty, too,—even were I not so well acquainted with your affairs,—that you would openly recognise me as your beloved wife in the face of the whole world, and would defy fate when in my arms, thus making me happy and blessed.

William IV to Caroline von Linsingen
(ca. 1791?)

But now, your heart, my property, is it given to another? From you alone will I learn all, from your lips hear the truth; *you* cannot deceive me. If you do not write, nothing shall hold, nothing bind me. I shall come and tear you from the altar; and who will dare to rob me of my wife?...

Your hand—how often has this heart beat under it with love, how often has it pressed mine own in ardent bliss— your hand, I say, alone can give me happiness or misery. I cannot yet grasp the incomprehensible. No, no, my wife's love is of the kind that lasts for ever! In the intoxication of our mutual passion we often felt that we had but one heart, one soul, that we were but one being, down to the veriest trifles; and is it possible that this should have an end? It was but three months ago that you could still embrace with burning fervour the tree in which I had cut our names, when I solemnly swore to you, my fondly loved, fondly loving maiden wife, to treat you as a sister so long as it was your wish; it was but two months ago that you fell down lifeless at the sudden sight of my portrait, that Dutton held before you; and now, you do but try to deceive yourself and me. But I know what all this must end in, and I live once again.

Let not my hope become my despair. Unloose the fetters. Be mine, or I shall curse even virtue herself—shall curse even you, and the sanctity of our love, and the power that your charms have over me. I shall curse myself that I did not enforce my legal rights with you, that I did not take what was already mine, so that I might never lose it again. Oh, wife, my wife, I am ever yours! Never shall another call your William husband!

Lady Caroline Lamb to Lord Byron
(1812)

The rose Lord Byron gave Lady Caroline Lamb died in despite of every effort made to save it; probably from regret at its fallen Fortunes. Hume, at least, who is no great believer in most things, says that many more die of broken hearts than is supposed. When Lady Caroline returns from Brocket Hall, she will dispatch the *Cabinet Maker* to Lord Byron, with the Flower she wishes most of all others to resemble, as, however deficient its beauty and even use, it has a noble and aspiring mind, and, having once beheld in its full lustre the bright and unclouded sun that for one moment condescended to shine upon it, never while it exists could it think any lower object worthy of its worship and Admiration. Yet the sunflower was punished for its temerity; but its fate is more to be envied than that of many less proud flowers. It is still superior to every other, and, though in this cold foggy atmosphere it meets no doubt with many disappointments, and though it never could, never will, have reason to boast of any peculiar mark of condescension or attention from the bright star to whom it pays constant homage, yet to behold it sometimes, to see it gazed at, to hear it admired, will repay all. She hopes, therefore, when brought by the little Page, it will be graciously received without any more Taunts and cuts about "Love of what is New."

Lady Caroline does not plead guilty to this most unkind charge, at least no further than is laudable, for that which is rare and is distinguished and singular ought to be more prized and sought after than what is commonplace and disagreeable. How can the other accusation, of being easily pleased, agree with this? The very circumstance of seeking out that which is of high value shows at least a mind not readily satisfied. But to attempt excuses for faults would be impossible with Lady Caroline. They have so long been rooted in a soil suited to their growth that a far less penetrating eye than Lord Byron's might perceive them— even on the shortest acquaintance. There is not one, however, though long indulged, that shall not be instantly got rid of, if Lord Byron thinks it worth while to name them. The reproof and abuse of some, however severe and just, may be valued more than the easily gained encomiums of the rest of the world.

Lord Byron to Lady Caroline Lamb
(1812)

My Dearest Caroline,

If the tears, which you saw, and know I am not apt to shed; if the agitation in which I parted from you—agitation which you must have perceived through the whole of this nervous affair, did not commence till the moment of leaving you approached; if all I have said and done, and am still but too ready to say and do, have not sufficiently proved what my feelings are, and must ever be, towards you, my love, I have no other proof to offer.

God knows I never knew till this moment the madness of my dear dearest and most beloved friend. I cannot express myself, this is no time for words—but I shall have a pride, a melancholy pleasure, in suffering what you yourself can scarcely conceive, for you do not know me.

I am about to go out with a heavy heart, for my appearing this evening will stop any absurd story to which the events of the day might give rise. Do you think now I am cold and stern and wilful? Will ever others think so? Will your mother ever? The mother to whom me must indeed sacrifice much more, much more on my part than she shall ever know, or can imagine.

Promise not to love you? Ah, Caroline, it is past promising! But I shall attribute all concessions to the proper motive, and never cease to feel all that you have already witnessed, and more than ever can be known, but to my own heart—perhaps, to yours. May God forgive, protect, and bless you ever and ever, more than ever.

Your most attached

BYRON

P.S.—These taunts have driven you to this, my dearest Caroline, and were it not for your mother, and the kindness of your connexions, is there anything in heaven or earth that would have made me so happy as to have made you mine long ago? And not less now than then, but more than ever *at this time*.

God knows I wish you happy, and when I quit you, or rather you, from a sense of duty to your husband and mother, quit me, you shall acknowledge the truth of what I again promise and vow, that no other, in word nor deed, shall ever hold the place in my affections which is and shall be sacred to you till I am nothing. You know I would with pleasure give up all here or beyond the grave for you, and in refraining from this must my motives be misunderstood?

I care not who knows this, what use is made of it—it is to you and to you only, yourself. I was, and am yours, freely and entirely, to obey, to honour, love, and fly with you, *when, where,* and *how,* yourself might and may determine.

Robert Browning to Elizabeth B. Barrett
(1845)

I love your verses with all my heart, dear Miss Barrett,—and this is no off-hand complimentary letter that I shall write,—whatever else, no prompt matter-of-course recognition of your genius, and there a graceful and natural end of the thing. Since the day last week when I first read your poems, I quite laugh to remember how I have been turning and turning again in my mind what I should be able to tell you of their effect upon me, for in the first flush of delight I thought I would this once get out of my habit of purely passive enjoyment, when I do really enjoy, and thoroughly justify my admiration—perhaps even, as a loyal fellow-craftsman should, try and find fault and do you some little good to be proud of hereafter!— but nothing comes of it all—so into me has it gone, and part of me has it become, this great living poetry of yours, not a flower of which but took root and grew—Oh, how different that is from lying to be dried and pressed flat, and prized highly, and put in a book with a proper account at top and bottom, and shut up and put away . . . and the book called a "Flora," besides! After all, I need not give up the thought of doing that, too, in time; because even now, talking with whoever is worthy, I can give a reason for my faith in one and another excellence, the fresh strange music, the affluent language, the exquisite pathos and true new brave thought; but in this addressing myself to you—your own self, and for the first time, my feeling rises altogether. I do, as I say, love these books with all my heart—and I love you too. Do you know I was once not very far from seeing—really seeing you? Mr. Kenyon said to me one morning

"Would you like to see Miss Barrett?" then he went to announce me,—then he returned...you were too unwell, and now it is years ago, and I feel as at some untoward passage in my travels, as if I had been close, so close, to some world's-wonder in chapel or crypt, only a screen to push and I might have entered, but there was some slight, so it now seems, slight and just sufficient bar to admission, and the half-opened door shut, and I went home my thousands of miles, and the sight was never to be?

Well, these Poems were to be, and this true thankful joy and pride with which I feel myself,

Yours ever faithfully,

ROBERT BROWNING

Elizabeth B. Barrett to Robert Browning
(1845)

I thank you, dear Mr. Browning, from the bottom of my heart. You meant to give me pleasure by your letter—and even if the object had not been answered, I ought still to thank you. But it is thoroughly answered. Such a letter from such a hand! Sympathy is dear—very dear to me: but the sympathy of a poet, and of such a poet, is the quintessence of sympathy to me! Will you take back my gratitude for it?—agreeing, too, that of all the commerce done in the world, from Tyre to Carthage, the exchange of sympathy for gratitude is the most princely thing!

For the rest you draw me on with your kindness. It is difficult to get rid of people when you once have given them too much pleasure—*that* is a fact, and we will not stop for the moral of it. What I was going to say—after a little natural hesitation—is, that if ever you emerge without inconvenient effort from your "passive state," and will tell me of such faults as rise to the surface and strike you as important in my poems, (for of course, I do not think of troubling you with criticism in detail) you will confer a lasting obligation on me, and one which I shall value so much, that I covet it at a distance. I do not pretend to any extraordinary meekness under criticism and it is possible enough that I might not be altogether obedient to yours. But with my high respect for your power in your Art and for your experience as an artist, it would be quite impossible for me to hear a general observation of yours on what appear to you my master-faults, without being the better for it hereafter in some way. I ask for only a sentence or two of general observation—and I do not ask even for *that*, so as to tease you—but in the humble, low voice, which is so excellent a thing in women—particularly when they go a-begging! The most frequent general criticism I receive, is, I think, upon the style, "if I *would* but change my style!" But *that* is an objection (isn't it?) to the writer bodily? Buffon says, and every sincere writer must feel, that "*Le style c'est l'homme*"; a fact, however, scarcely calculated to lessen the objection with certain critics.

Is it indeed true that I was so near to the pleasure and honour of making your acquaintance? and can it be true that you look back upon the lost opportunity with any regret? *But*—you know—if you had entered the "crypt," you might have caught cold, or been tired to death, and *wished* yourself "a thousand miles off"; which would have been worse than travelling them. It is not my interest, however, to put such thoughts in your head about its being "all for the best"; and I would rather hope (as I do) that what I lost by one chance I may recover by some future one. Winters shut me up as they do dormouse's eyes; in the spring, *we shall see*: and I am so much better that I seem turning round to the outward world again. And in the meantime I have learnt to know your voice, not merely from the poetry but from the kindness in it. Mr. Kenyon often speaks of you—dear Mr. Kenyon!—who most unspeakably, or only speakably with tears in my eyes,—has been my friend and helper, and my book's friend and helper! critic and sympathiser, true friend of all hours! You know him well enough, I think, to understand that I must be grateful to him.

I am writing too much,—and notwithstanding that I am writing too much, I will write of one thing more. I will say that I am your debtor, not only for this cordial letter and for all the pleasure which came with it, but in other ways, and those the highest: and I will say that while I live to follow this divine art of poetry, in proportion to my love for it and my devotion to it, I must be a devout admirer and student of your works. This is in my heart to say to you—and I say it.

And, for the rest, I am proud to remain

Your obliged and faithful

ELIZABETH B. BARRETT

LONG-
DISTANCE
LOVE

Henry VIII to Anne Boleyn
(ca. 1528?)

My Mistress and Friend,

My heart and I surrender ourselves into your hands, beseeching you to hold us commended to your favour, and that by absence your affection to us may not be lessened; for it were a great pity to increase our pain, of which absence produces enough and more than I could ever have thought could be felt, reminding us of a point in astronomy which is this: the longer the days are, the more distant is the sun, and nevertheless the hotter. So is it with our love, for by absence we are kept a distance from one another, and yet it retains its fervour, at least on my side; I hope the like on yours, assuring you that on my part the pain of absence is already too great for me. And when I think of the increase of that which I am forced to suffer, it would be almost intolerable, but for the firm hope I have of your unchangeable affection for me; and to remind you of this sometimes, and seeing that I cannot be personally present with you, I now send you the nearest thing I can to that, namely, my picture set in a bracelet, with the whole of the device, which you already know, wishing myself in their place, if it should please you.

This is from the hand of your loyal servant and friend,

H. R.

Katherine Parr to Henry VIII
(ca. 1544?)

Although the distance of time and account of days neither is long nor many of your Majesty's absence, yet the want of your presence, so much desired and beloved by me, maketh me that I cannot quietly pleasure in anything until I hear from your Majesty. The time, therefore, seemeth to me very long, with a great desire to know how your Highness hath done since your departing hence, whose prosperity and health I desire more than mine own. And whereas I know your Majesty's absence is never without great need, yet love and affection compel me to desire your presence.

Again, the same zeal and affection forceth me to be best content with that which is your will and pleasure. Thus love maketh me in all things to set apart mine own convenience and pleasure, and to embrace most joyfully his will and pleasure whom I love. God, the knower of secrets, can judge these words not to be written only with ink, but most truly impressed on the heart. Much more I omit, lest it be thought I go about to praise myself, or crave a thank; which thing to do I mind nothing less but a plain, simple relation of the love and zeal I bear your Majesty, proceeding from the abundance of the heart. Wherein I must confess I desire no commendation, having such just occasion to do the same.

I make like account with your Majesty as I do with God for his benefits and gifts heaped upon me daily, acknowledging myself a great debtor to him, not being able to recompense the least of His benefits; in which state I am certain and sure to die, yet I hope in his gracious acceptance of my good will. Even such confidence have I in your Majesty's gentleness, knowing myself never to have done my duty as were requisite and meet for such a noble prince, at whose hands I have found and received so much love and goodness that with words I cannot express it.

Lest I should be too tedious to your Majesty, I finish this my scribbled letter, committing you to the governance of the Lord, with long and prosperous life here, and after this life to enjoy the kingdom of his elect.

From Greenwich, by your Majesty's humble and obedient wife and servant,

KATERYN THE QUEEN

Henry of Navarre to Corisande D'Andouins (1588)

Dear heart, I am more a man of action than of thought. Your last message reproved me for my lost diligence in writing. Every night I read your letter. If I love it, what ought I to do toward her whence it came? Never have I had such longing to see you. If the enemy does not press us after this present victory, I shall steal away for a month.

Kate, Duchess of Buckingham, to Her Husband, George Villiers, Duke of Buckingham (1623)

My dear Lord,

I humbly thank you that you were pleased to write so many letters to me, which was so great a comfort to me as you cannot imagine, for I protest to God I have had a grievous time of this our grievous parting, for I am sure it has been so to me, and my heart has felt enough more than I hope it ever shall do again; and I pray God release me out of it by your speedy coming hither again to her that doth as dearly love you as ever woman did man; and if everybody did love you but a quarter as well, you were the happiest man that ever was born, but that is impossible. But I protest I think you are the best beloved that ever favourite was, for all that have true worth in them cannot but love your sweet disposition. If I were not so near to you as I thank God I am, I could say no less, if I said truth, for I think there never was such a man born as you are; and how much am I bound to God that I must be that happy woman, to enjoy you from all other women,—I, the unworthiest of all, to have so great a blessing! Only this I can say for myself, you could never have had one that could love you better than your poor, true loving Kate doth, poor now in your absence, but else the happiest and richest woman in the world. I thank you for your long letter; I think I must give Sir Francis Cottington thanks for it too, because you say he bade you write long letters. I am beholden to him for that, because I am sure he knew they could never be *too* long for me, for it is all the comfort I have now to read often over your letters. My reason that I desired you not to do it was for fear of troubling you too much; but, since you think it none, I am much bound to you for it, and I beseech you to continue it.

John Churchill, Duke of Marlborough, to Sarah, Duchess of Marlborough
(1709)

I do hope this winter will put an end to this war, and that the peace may last as long as we shall live; and I do assure you I long every day to be more and more with you, to live as happily as our circumstances will permit, not to affect the meddling with public business, by which I hope we may be eased both of envy and trouble.

David Hume to Madame de Boufflers
(1766)

It is impossible for me, dear madam, to express the difficulty which I have to bear your absence, and the continual want which I feel of your society. I had accustomed myself, of a long time, to think of you as a friend from whom I was never to be separated during any considerable time; and I had flattered myself that we were peculiarly fitted to pass our lives in intimacy and cordiality with each other. Age and a natural equality of temper were in danger of reducing my heart to too great indifference about everything, it was enlivened by the charms of your conversation, and the vivacity of your character. Your mind, more agitated both by unhappy circumstances in your situation and by your natural disposition, could repose itself in the more calm sympathy which you found with me.

But behold! three months are elapsed since I left you; and it is impossible for me to assign a time when I can hope to join you. I still return to my wish, that I had never left Paris, and that I had kept out of the reach of all other duties, except that which was so sweet, and agreeable, to fulfil, the cultivating your friendship and enjoying your society. Your obliging expressions revive this regret in the strongest degree; especially where you mention the wounds which, though skinned over, still fester at the bottom.

Oh! my dear friend, how I dread that it may still be long ere you reach a state of tranquillity, in a distress which so little admits of any remedy, and which the natural elevation of your character, instead of putting you above it, makes you feel with greater sensibility. I could only wish to administer the temporary consolation, which the presence of a friend never fails to afford...I kiss your hands with all the devotion possible.

Marquis de Lafayette to His Wife,
Madame de Lafayette
(1777)

I am writing to you from a great distance, my dearest love, and, in addition to this painful circumstance, I feel also the still more dreadful uncertainty of the time when I may receive any news of you. I hope, however, soon to have a letter from you; and among the various reasons which render me so desirous of a speedy arrival this is the one which excites in me the greatest degree of impatience. How many fears and anxieties enhance the keen anguish I feel at being separated from all that I love most fondly in the world! How have you borne my second departure? Have you loved me less? Have you forgiven me? Have you reflected that at all events I must equally have been parted from you—wandering about in Italy, dragging on an inglorious life, surrounded by the persons most opposed to my projects and to my manner of thinking? All these reflections did not prevent my experiencing the most bitter grief when the moment arrived for quitting my native shore. Your sorrow, that of my friends, Henrietta* all rushed upon my thoughts, and my heart was torn by a thousand painful feelings. I could not at that instant find any excuse for my own conduct. If you could know all that I have suffered, and the melancholy days that I have passed, while thus flying from all that I love best in the world! Must I join to this affliction the grief of hearing that you do not forgive me? It should in truth, my love, be too unhappy.

*His firstborn

Portia Adams to Her Husband, John Adams
(1782)

I look back to the early days of our acquaintance and friendship as to the days of love and innocence, and, with an indescribable pleasure, I have seen near a score of years roll over our heads with an affection heightened and improved by time, nor have the dreary years of absence in the smallest degree effaced from my mind the image of the dear untitled man to whom I gave my heart. I cannot sometimes refrain considering the honours with which he is invested as badges of my unhappiness. The unbounded confidence I have in your attachment to me and to the dear pledges of our affection, has soothed the solitary hours and rendered your absence more supportable, for had I loved you with the same affection, it must have been misery to have doubted. Yet a cruel world too often injures my feelings by wondering how a person, possessed of domestic attachments, can sacrifice them by absenting himself for years.

"If you had known," said a person to me the other day, "that Mr. Adams would have remained so long abroad, would you have consented that he should have gone?" I recollected myself a moment, and then spoke the real dictates of my heart. "If I had known, sir, that Mr. Adams could have effected what he has done, I would not only have submitted to the absence I have endured, painful as it has been, but I would not have opposed it even though three years more should be added to the number (which Heaven avert). I feel a pleasure in being able to sacrifice my selfish passions to the general good, and in imitating the example which has taught me to consider myself and family but as the small dust in the balance when compared with the great community."

It is now, my dear friend, a long, long time since I have had a line from you. The fate of Gibraltar leads me to fear that a peace is far distant, and that I shall see you—God only knows when. I shall say little about my former request; not that my desire is less, but, before this can reach you, 'tis probable I may receive your opinion: if in favour of my coming to you, I shall have no occasion to urge it further; if against it, I will not embarrass you by again requesting it. I will endeavour to sit down and consider it as the portion allotted to me.

Adieu, my dear friend. Why is it that I hear so seldom from my dear John? But one letter have I ever received from him since he arrived in Petersburg. I wrote him by the last opportunity. Ever remember me, as I do you, with all the tenderness which it is possible for one object to feel for another, which no time can obliterate, no distance alter, but which is always the same in the bosom of

PORTIA

Aaron Burr to His Wife, Theodosia
(1793)

I received with joy and astonishment, on entering the Senate this minute, your two elegant and affectionate letters. The mail closes in a few minutes, and will scarce allow me to acknowledge your goodness. The roads and ferries have been for some days almost impassable, so that till now no post has arrived since Monday.

It was a knowledge of your mind which first inspired me with a respect for that of your sex, and with some regret, I confess, that the ideas which you have often heard me express in favour of female intellectual powers are founded on what I have imagined more than on what I have seen, *except in you.* I have endeavoured to trace the causes of this rare display of genius in women, and find them in the errors of education, of prejudice, and of habit. I admit that men are equally, nay more, much more to blame than women. Boys and girls are generally educated much in the same way till they are eight or nine years of age, and it is admitted the girls make at least equal progress with the boys; generally, indeed, they make better. Why, then, has it never been thought worth the attempt to discover, by fair experiment, the particular age at which the male superiority becomes so evident? But this is not in answer to your letter; neither is it possible now to answer it. Some parts of it I shall never answer. . . . Your plan and embellishment of my mode of life are fanciful, are flattering and inviting; we will endeavour to realize some of it. Pray continue to write, if you can do so with impunity. I bless Sir J., who, with the assistance of Heaven, has thus far restored you.

In the course of this scrawl I have been several times called to vote, and must apologize to you for its incoherence. Adieu.

A. BURR

Mary Wollstonecraft to Captain Gilbert Imlay
(1793)

How are you? I have been following you all along the road this comfortless weather; for when I am absent from those I love, my imagination is as lively as if my senses had never been gratified by their presence—I was going to say caresses; and why should I not?

I have found that I have more mind than you in one respect; because I can, without any violent effort of reason, find food for love in the same object much longer than you can. The way to my senses is through my heart; but, forgive me! I think there is sometimes a shorter cut to yours.

With ninety-nine men out of a hundred, a very sufficient dash of folly is necessary to render a woman *piquante*, a soft word for desirable; and, beyond these casual ebullitions of sympathy, few look for enjoyment by fostering a passion in their hearts. One reason, in short, why I wish my whole sex to become wiser is, that the foolish ones may not, by their pretty folly, rob those whose sensibility keeps down their vanity, of the few roses that afford them some solace in the thorny road of life.

I do not know how I fell into these reflections, excepting one thought produced it,—that these continual separations were necessary to warm your affection. Of late we are always separating. Crack! crack! and away you go! This joke wears the sallow cast of thought; for, though I began to write cheerfully, some melancholy tears have found their way into my eyes that linger there, whilst a glow of tenderness at my heart whispers that you are one of the best creatures in the world. Pardon, then, the vagaries of a mind that has been almost "crazed by care," as well as "crossed in hapless love," and bear with me a little longer. When we are settled in the country together, more duties will open before me, and my heart, which now, trembling into peace, is agitated by every emotion that awakens the remembrance of old griefs, will learn to rest on yours with that dignity your character, not to mention my own, demands.

Take care of yourself, and write soon to your own girl (you may add dear, if you please), who sincerely loves you, and will try to convince you of it by becoming happier.

MARY

Napoleon Bonaparte to His Wife, Josephine (1796)

I have received all your letters [from Paris], but none has affected me like the last. How can you think, my charmer, of writing to me in such terms? Do you think my position is not already painful enough without further increasing my regrets and subverting my reason? What eloquence, what feeling you display; they are of fire, they inflame my poor heart! My only

Josephine, away from you there is no more joy—away from you the world is a wilderness in which I stand alone, and without knowing the bliss of unburdening my soul. You have robbed me of more than my soul; you are the one thought of my life. When I am weary of the worries of my profession, when I mistrust the issue, when men disgust me, when I am ready to curse my life, I put my hand on my heart where your portrait lies.

By what art have you learnt how to captivate all my faculties, to concentrate in yourself my spiritual existence—it is witchery, dear love, which will end only with me. To live for Josephine, that is the history of my life. I am struggling to get near you, I am dying to be by your side; fool that I am, I fail to realise how far off I am, that countries and provinces separate us. What an age it will be before you read these lines, the weak expressions of the fevered soul in which you reign. Ah, my winsome wife, I know not what fate awaits me, but if it keeps me much longer from you it will be unbearable—my strength will not last. There was a time in which I prided myself on my strength, and, sometimes, when casting my eyes on the ills which men might do me, on the fate that destiny might have in store for me, I have gazed steadfastly on the most incredible misfortunes without a wrinkle on my brow or a vestige of surprise. But today the thought that my Josephine might be ill, and, above all, the cruel, the fatal thought that she might love me less, blights my soul, stops my pulse, makes me wretched and dejected, without even leaving me the courage of fury and despair. I often used to say that men have no power over him who dies without regrets; but today, to die without your love, to die in uncertainty of that, is the torment of hell, it is a lifelike and terrifying figure of absolute annihilation—I feel passion strangling me. My only friend companion! you whom fate has destined to walk with me the painful path of life! the day on which I no longer possess your heart will be that on which parched nature will be without warmth and without vegetation for me. I stop, dear love! My soul is sad, my body tired, my spirit dazed, men worry me—I ought indeed to detest them; they keep me from my beloved.

I am at Port Maurice, near Oneille; tomorrow I shall be at Albenga. The two armies are in motion. We are trying to deceive each other—victory to the cleverest! I am pretty well satisfied with Beaulieu; he would needs be a much stronger man than his predecessor to alarm me much. I expect to give him a good drubbing. Don't be anxious. Love me as thine eyes, but that is not enough—as thyself, more than thyself—as thy thoughts, thy mind, thy sight, thy all. Dear love, forgive me, I am exhausted; nature is weak for him who feels acutely, for him whom you inspire.

N. B.

Percy Shelley to Mary Wollstonecraft Godwin (1814)

Oh! my dearest love, why are our pleasures so short and so interrupted? How long is this to last?

Know you, my best Mary, that I feel myself, in your absence, almost degraded to the level of the vulgar and impure. I feel their vacant, stiff eyeballs fixed upon me, until I seem to have been infected with their loathsome meaning—to inhale a sickness that subdues me to languor. Oh! those redeeming eyes of Mary, that they might beam upon me before I sleep! Praise my forbearance—oh! beloved one—that I do not rashly fly to you, and at least secure a moment's bliss. Wherefore should I delay; do you not long to meet me? All that is exalted and buoyant in my nature urges me towards you, reproaches me with the cold delay, laughs at all fear and spurns to dream of prudence. Why am I not with you?

Mary Wollstonecraft Godwin to Percy Shelley
(1814)

Good-night, my love; to-morrow I will seal this blessing on your lips. Dear, good creature, press me to you, and hug your own Mary to your heart. Perhaps she will one day have a father: till then be everything to me, love, and, indeed, I will be a good girl and never vex you. I will learn Greek, and—but when shall we meet when I may tell you all this, and you will so sweetly reward me? Oh! we must meet soon, for this is a dreary life. I am weary of it: a poor widowed deserted thing, no one cares for her; but ah, love, is not that enough? I have a very sincere affection for my Shelley. But good-night; I am wofully tired and sleepy. Sleeping I shall dream of you, ten to one, when you, naughty one, have quite forgotten me. Take me—one kiss—well, that is enough. To-morrow!

Helmuth von Moltke to Mary Burt
(1841)

How much I long, dearest Mary, to hear again from you soon! Perhaps another letter from you is on the way; I will not wait for it, however, but will at once start another little talk with you. The full moon is shining right into my window; you will see it, too, today, no doubt. I wish it were a mirror, so that I could see your dear sweet features in it, and your nut-brown eyes and soft smiling mouth. Close by is the large star I wrote to you about. Often in the far-away Asiatic plains, when I had been riding all through the hot day, and night fell before the tired horses had reached their quarters, or when I had my carpet spread for a couch on the flat roof of my dwelling-place, this bright star used to make its appearance towards the south in the sunset glow, and, shining softly, seemed to say, "Ride in peace, and forget all care, you will yet find a heart that will love you!" And now I have found you, dear Mary; but the star of fate is in one's own breast, and everyone is as happy as he deserves to be. If I should not be so with you it would be because I am not so pure and good as you, and can never become so. The longer I live the more clearly I see that, even in this life, both good and evil bring their just recompense, with but few exceptions. And so, whatever your life may be outwardly, you will always have the happiness of inward peace, for you are like a flower, lovely, gentle, and pure, and I pray God that He may keep you so.…

MAD
LOVE

Henry of Navarre to Gabriella D'Estrées
(1593)

I am impatient if a day passes without news of you. It seems like an eternity. But what can I say of the second day, when I discover that my enemies had captured my messenger, when I had attributed the delay to you? I was wrong to blame you, my angel, when I was so certain of your affection, which indeed is my due, for never was my love greater and my passion more violent, so that I cease not to repeat in all my letters: come, come, come, my dear love, honour with your presence the one who, if he were free, would go a thousand miles, and throw himself at your feet, and so prevent them moving.

Thomas Otway to Elizabeth Barry
(ca. 1678?)

My Tyrant,

I endure too much torment to be silent, and have endured it too long not to make the severest complaint. I love you; I dote on you; my love makes me mad when I am near you, and despair when I am from you. Sure, of all miseries love is to me the most intolerable; it haunts me in my sleep, perplexes me when waking; every melancholy thought makes my fears more powerful, and every delightful one makes my wishes more unruly. In all other uneasy chances of a man's life, there's an immediate recourse to some kind of succour or another: in want, we apply to our friends; in sickness, to physicians; but love—the sum, the total of all misfortunes— must be endured in silence; no friend so dear to trust with such a secret, nor remedy in art so powerful to remove its anguish. Since the first day I saw you I have hardly enjoyed one day of perfect quiet. I loved you early; and no sooner had I beheld that bewitching face of yours than I felt in my heart the very foundation of all my peace give way; but when you became another's, I must confess that I did then rebel,—had foolish pride enough to promise myself that I would recover my liberty, in spite of my enslaved nature; I swore against myself I would not love you; I affected a resentment, stifled my spirit, and would not let it bend so much as once to upbraid you. Each day it was my chance to see or be near you; with stubborn sufferance I resolved to bear and brave your power,—nay, *did* it too, often successfully. Generally, with wine or conversation I diverted or appeased the demon that possessed me; but when at night, returning to my unhappy self, to give my heart an account why I had done it so unnatural a violence, it was then I always paid a treble interest for the short moments of ease which I had borrowed; then every treacherous thought rose up, nor left me till they had thrown me on my bed, and opened those sluices of tears that were to flow till morning. This has been for some years my best condition; nay, time itself, that decays all things else, has but increased and added to my longings. I tell you, and charge you to believe it as you are generous (which sure you must be, for everything except your neglect of me persuades me you are so), even at this time, though other arms have held you, that I love you with that tenderness of spirit, that purity of truth, that sincerity of heart, that I could sacrifice the nearest friends or interests I have on earth barely to please you. If I had all the world, it should be yours; for with it I could but be miserable, were you not mine.

I appeal to yourself for justice, if through the whole actions of my life I have done any one thing that might not let you see how absolute your authority was over me. Your commands have been sacred to me; your smiles have transported, your frowns awed me. In short, you will quickly become to me the greatest blessing or the greatest curse that ever man was doomed to. I cannot so much as look on you without confusion. You only can, with the healing cordial *love*, assuage and calm my torments. Pity the man, then, that would be proud to die for you, and cannot live without you, and allow him thus far to boast that you never were beloved by a creature that had a nobler or juster pretence to your heart than the

Unfortunate

O<small>TWAY</small>

William Congreve to Mrs. Arabella Hunt
(ca. 1690?)

Dear Madam,

Not believe that I love you? You cannot pretend to be so incredulous. If you do not believe my tongue, consult my eyes, consult your own. You will find by yours that they have charms; by mine that I have a heart which feels them. Recall to mind what happened last night. That at least was a lover's kiss. Its eagerness, its fierceness, its warmth, expressed the God its parent. But oh! its sweetness, and its melting softness expressed him more. With trembling in my limbs and fevers in my soul I ravish'd it. Convulsions, pantings, murmurings shew'd the mighty disorder within me: the mighty disorder increased by it. For those dear lips shot through my heart, and thro' my bleeding vitals, delicious poison, and an avoidless but yet a charming ruin.

What cannot a day produce? The night before I thought myself a happy man, in want of nothing, and in fairest expectation of fortune; approved of by men of wit, and applauded by others—pleased, nay charmed with my friends, my then dearest friends, sensible of every delicate pleasure, and in their turns possessing all.

But Love, almighty Love, seems in a moment to have removed me to a prodigious distance from every object but you alone. In the midst of crowds I remain in solitude. Nothing but you can lay hold of my mind, and that can lay hold of nothing but you. I appear transported to some foreign desert with you (oh, that I were really thus transported!), where, abundantly supplied with everything, in thee I might live out an age of uninterrupted extasy.

The scene of the world's great stage seems suddenly and sadly chang'd. Unlovely objects are all around me, excepting thee; the charms of all the world appear to be translated to thee. Thus in this sad but oh, too pleasing state! my soul can fix upon nothing but thee; thee it contemplates, admires, adores, nay depends on, trusts on you alone.

If you and hope forsake it, despair and endless misery attend it.

Richard Steele to Mary Scurlock
(1707)

Madam,

With what language shall I address my lovely fair, to acquaint her with the sentiments of a heart she delights to torture? I have not a minute's quiet out of your sight; and when I am with you, you use me with so much distance that I am still in a state of absence, heightened with a view of the charms which I am denied to approach. In a word, you must give me either a fan, a mask, or a glove you have worn, or I cannot live; otherwise you must expect that I'll kiss your hand, or, when I next sit by you, steal your handkerchief. You yourself are too great a bounty to be received at once; therefore I must be prepared by degrees, lest the mighty gift distract me with joy. Dear Mrs. Scurlock, I am tired with calling you by that name; therefore, say the day in which you will take that of, Madam,

Your most obedient, most devoted humble servant,

RICH. STEELE

Alexander Pope to Lady Mary Wortley Montagu
(1718)

Madam,

I have been (what I never was till now) in debt to you for a letter some weeks.... I long for nothing so much as your Oriental self. You must of necessity be *advanced* so far *back* into true nature and simplicity of manner, by these three years' residence in the East, that I shall look upon you as so many years younger than you was, so much nearer innocence (that is, truth) and infancy (that is, openness).

I expect to see your soul as much thinner dressed as your body; and that you have left off, as unwieldy and cumbersome, a great many European habits.

Without offence to your modesty be it spoken, I have a burning desire to see your soul stark naked, for I am confident it is the prettiest kind of white soul in the universe. But, if I forget whom I am talking to; you may possibly by this time believe, according to the prophet, that you have none; if so, show me that which comes next to a soul—I mean your heart. But I must be content with seeing your body only, God send it to come quickly. I honour it more than the diamond-casket that held Homer's Iliads; for in the very twinkle of one eye of it there is more wit, and in the very dimple of one cheek of it there is more meaning, than all the souls that ever were casually put into women since men had the making of them....

Pray let me hear from you soon, though I shall very soon write again. I am confident half our letters are lost.

Hester Vanhomrigh to Jonathan Swift
(1720)

Put my passion under the utmost restraint, send me as distant from you as the earth will allow, yet you cannot banish those charming ideas which will ever stick by me whilst I have the use of memory. Nor is the love I bear you only seated in my soul, for there is not a single atom of my frame that is not blended with it; therefore don't flatter yourself that separation will ever change my sentiments, for I find myself unquiet in the midst of silence, and my heart at once pierced with sorrow and love. For Heaven's sake, tell me what has caused this prodigious change in you which I have found of late. If you have the least remains of pity for me left, tell me tenderly. No; *don't* tell it, so that it may cause my present death, and don't suffer me to live a life like a languishing death, which is the only life I can lead if you have lost any of your tenderness for me.

Madame de Favras to Marquis de Favras
(1790)

My heart is intoxicated with its love for you. Never has anyone loved as I love you; and I repeat to you, with rapture, that I will devote each moment of my life to prove my affection. Remember that I cannot live apart from you, that the whole universe is nothing for me without you, without my love, without yours; but remember also that I would rather mourn your death than be ashamed of your life. I speak in the name of your children; never forget them in any circumstances of your life; if it were necessary, they would help to keep up your courage.

The Duke of Sussex to Lady Augusta Murray
(1793)

Will you allow me to come this evening? It is my only hope. Oh, let me come, and we will send for Mr. Gunn. Everything but this is hateful to me. More than forty-eight hours have I passed without the smallest nourishment. Oh, let me not live so. Death is certainly better than this; which, if in forty-eight hours it has not taken place, must follow; for, by all that is holy, till when I am married, I will eat nothing; and if I am not to be married the promise shall die with me! I am resolute. Nothing in the world shall alter my determination. If Gunn will not marry me I will die. . . . I will be conducted in everything by you; but I must be married, or die. I would rather see none of my family than be deprived of you. You alone can make me; you alone shall this evening. I will sooner drop than give you up. Good God! how I feel! and my love to be doubted sincere and warm. The Lord knows the truth of it; and as I say, if in forty-eight hours I am not married, I am no more. Oh, Augusta, my soul, let us try; let me come; I am capable of everything; I fear nothing, and Mr. Gunn, seeing our resolution, will agree. I am half dead. Good God! what will become of me? I shall go mad, most undoubtedly.

Napoleon Bonaparte to His Wife, Josephine
(1796)

My life is a perpetual nightmare. A presentiment of ill oppresses me. I see you no longer. I have lost more than life, more than happiness, more than my rest. I am almost without hope. I hasten to send a courier to you. He will stay only four hours in Paris, and then bring me your reply. Write me ten pages. That alone can console me a little. You are ill, you love me, I have made you unhappy, you are in delicate health, and I do not see you! These thoughts overwhelm me. I have done you so much wrong that I know not how to atone for it; I accuse you of staying in Paris, and you were ill there. Forgive me, my dear; the love with which you have inspired me has bereft me of reason. I shall never find it again. It is a disease for which there is no cure. My presentiments are so ominous that I would confine myself to merely seeing you, to pressing you for two hours to my heart—and then dying with you....

I am nothing without you. I scarcely imagine how I existed without knowing you. Ah, Josephine, had you known my heart would you have waited from May 18th to June 4th before starting? Would you have given an ear to perfidious friends who are perhaps desirous of keeping you away from me? I openly avow it to everyone: I hate everybody who is near you. I expected you to set out on May 25th, and arrive on June 3rd....

In your letter, dear, be sure to tell me that you are convinced that I love you more than it is possible to imagine; that you are persuaded that all my moments are consecrated to you; that to think of any other woman has never entered my head—they are all in my eyes without grace, wit, or beauty; that you, you alone, such as I see you, such as you are, can please me, and absorb all the faculties of my mind; that you have traversed its whole extent; that my heart has no recess into which you have not seen, no thoughts which are not subordinate to yours; that my strength, my prowess, my spirit are all yours; that my soul is in your body; and that the day on which you change or cease to live will be my death-day; that nature, that earth, is beautiful only because you dwell therein. If you do not believe all this, if your soul is not convinced, penetrated by it, you grieve me, you do not love me,—there is a magnetic fluid between people who love one another,—you know perfectly well that I could not brook a rival, would not endure one. To see him and tear out his heart would be for me the one and same thing, and then if I were to lift my hands against your sacred person—no, I should never dare to do it; but I would quit a life in which the most virtuous of women had deceived me.

But I am sure and proud of your love; misfortunes are the trials which reveal to each mutually the whole force of our passion. A child as charming as its mother will soon see the daylight, and will pass many years in your arms. Hapless I! ...

Laurence Sterne to Elizabeth Lumley
(ca. 1839?)

Yes! I will steal from the world, and not a babbling tongue shall tell where I am. Echo shall not so much as whisper my hiding-place. Suffer thy imagination to paint it as a little sun-gilt cottage, on the side of a romantic hill. Dost thou think I will leave love and friendship behind me? No! they shall be my companions in solitude, for they will sit down and rise up with me in the amiable form of my L——. We will be as merry and as innocent as our first parents in Paradise, before the arch-fiend entered that indescribable scene.

The kindest affections will have room to shoot and expand in our retirement, and produce such fruit as madness and envy and ambition have always killed in the bud. Let the human tempest and hurricane rage at a distance, the desolation is beyond the horizon of peace. My L —— has seen a polyanthus blow in December—some friendly wall has sheltered it from the biting wind. No planetary influence shall reach us but that which presides and cherishes the sweetest flowers. God preserve us! How delightful this prospect in idea! We will build and we will plant, in our way—simplicity shall not be tortured by art. We will learn of nature how to live—she shall be our alchemist, to mingle all the good of life in one salubrious draught. The gloomy family of care and distrust shall be banished from our dwelling, guarded by the kind and tutelar deity. We will sing our choral songs of gratitude and rejoice to the end of our pilgrimage.

Adieu, my L ——. Return to one who languishes for thy society.

L. STERNE

Prosper Mérimée to "Unknown"
(1841)

You take me for angel and devil—principally the latter. You call me tempter. Dare you say that this word does not apply much better to you than to me? Have you not thrown a bait to me, poor little fish that I am? And now, that you hold me on your hook, you make me dance between heaven and water just to please you, and when you are tired with the sport you will cut the line. Then I shall have a hook in my mouth—and shall never find another fisher.

Honoré de Balzac to Madame Hanska
(Countess Evelina Rzewuska)
(1845)

I went to fetch the finished proofs of "The Middle Classes." The printing office where they are being set in type is close by Saint-Germain-des-Prés. The thought took me to enter the church, where a cupola is being painted, and I prayed for you and for your dear child before the altar of the Virgin. Tears came into my eyes as I prayed to God to preserve you both in health and life. My thought shed its rays as far as the Neva; on returning to earth, perhaps, I may have brought with me some faint reflex from the Throne before which we both of us worship. With what fervour, and warmth, and self-abandonment I feel myself bound to you for ever—for time and for eternity, as the pious say.

As I returned I bought on the quay, for fifteen sous, the "Memoirs of Lauzun," which I had never read. I glanced through the book in the omnibus, on the road to Passy, where on arrival your slave once more took to the arm-chair whence he now writes to you, while waiting for dinner. How strange it is that a fine courageous fellow, a man who seems not to have been wanting in good feeling on occasion, should so lightly dishonour the woman he professes to have loved! I believe vanity, being the dominant side of his character, stifled all that was really good and generous in him.

After having read and closed this bad book, I exclaimed to myself, What happiness it is to love one woman only! This is both a heart-felt expression and the result of reasoning and observation; for I can analyse you with the most perfect coolness, and I perceive with glad conviction that no one can be compared to you. I know not in the world such another perfect intelligence, a more noble heart, a more sweet and charming temper, a more upright character, a sounder judgment, nor anyone who is so wise and reasonable. I could say more, only I am afraid of being scolded, yet all this justifies and explains the impulse, stronger to-day even than in 1833, that makes my heart beat at the sight of a page of your "Toppfer," which will lie on my table for the rest of my days, and my delight at the sight of the miniature.

Ah! you do not know all I felt when—at the end of that court, the smallest pebbles of which remain enshrined in my memory as well as the long flower-beds and the coach houses—I first saw your sweet face at the window. I lost all consciousness of being in the body, and when I spoke to you I was stupefied. This stupefaction lasted for two days, and then the torrent, stopped in its course, only dashed on with gathered force. "What must she think of me?" was the mad phrase which I repeated again and again in utter terror.

No, it is true; and you must believe me when I say that even yet, after all these years, I have not become accustomed to knowing you. Centuries would not suffice, and life is so short! You saw the fact in those two months. I was in the same state of ecstasy and bewilderment when I went away as I was the first day I beheld you.

Heinrich Heine to the "Fly" (Elise Krinitz) (1855)

I shall be delighted to see you again, my graceful little musk-cat; you are as dainty as an Angora cat, the sort I have always had a fancy for. At one time I had a leaning toward tiger-cats, but they are too dangerous, and they sometimes left an unpleasant living impress upon my face. I am still very ill, and the annoyances with which I am constantly harried make my health still worse—as if it were not hopeless enough already. I am a dying man, thirsting for the wildest delights that life has to offer. It is horrible!

Edgar Allan Poe to Mrs. Sarah Helen Whitman
(1848)

I have pressed your letter again and again to my lips, sweetest Helen—bathing it in tears of joy, or of a "divine despair." But I—who so lately, in your presence, vaunted the "power of words"—of what avail are mere words to me now? *Could* I believe in the efficiency of prayer to the God of Heaven, I would indeed kneel—humbly kneel—at this the most earnest epoch of my life—kneel in entreaty for words—*but* for words that should disclose to you—that might enable me to lay bare to you my whole heart. All thoughts—all passions seem now merged in that one consuming desire—the mere wish to make you comprehend—to make you see *that* for which there is no human voice—the unutterable fervour of my love for you:—for so well do I know your poet nature, that I feel sure if you could but look down *now* into the depths of my soul with your pure spiritual eyes you *could* not refuse to speak to me what, alas! you still resolutely leave unspoken—you would *love* me if only for the greatness of my love. Is it not something in this cold, dreary world *to be loved*? Oh, if I could but burn into your spirit the deep—the *true* meaning which I attach to those three syllables underlined! but, alas! the effort is all in vain and "I live and die unheard." . . .

Could I but have held you close to my heart and whispered to you the strange secrets of its passionate history, then indeed you would have seen that it was not and never could have been in the power of any other than yourself to move me as I am now moved—to oppress me with this ineffable emotion—to surround and bathe me in this electric light, illumining and enkindling my whole nature—filling my soul with glory, with wonder, and with awe. During our walk in the cemetery I said to you, while the bitter, bitter tears sprang into my eyes, "Helen, I love now—now—for the first and only time." I said this, I repeat, in no hope that you could believe me, but because I could not help feeling how unequal were the heart riches we might offer each to each:—I, for the first time, giving my all at once and for ever, even while the words of your poem were yet ringing in my ears.

Ah, Helen, *why* did you show them to me? There seemed, too, so very especial a purpose in what you did. Their very beauty was cruelty *to me....*

And now, in the most simple words I can command, let me paint to you the impression made upon me by your personal presence. As you entered the room, pale, hesitating, and evidently oppressed at heart; as your eyes rested for one brief moment upon mine, I felt, for the first time in my life, and tremblingly acknowledged, the existence of spiritual influences altogether out of the reach of the reason. I saw that you were *Helen*—my Helen—the Helen of a thousand dreams. . . . She whom the Great Giver of all good had preordained to be mine—mine only—if not now, alas! then hereafter and *for ever* in the Heavens.—You spoke falteringly and seemed scarcely conscious of what you said. I heard no words—only the soft voice more familiar to me than my own....

Your hand rested within mine and my whole soul shook with a tremulous ecstacy: and then, but for the fear of grieving or wounding you, I would have fallen at your feet in as pure—in as real a worship as was ever offered to Idol or to God.

And when, afterwards, on those two successive evenings of all-heavenly delight, you passed to and fro about the room—now sitting by my side, now far away, now standing with your hand resting on the back of my chair, while the preternatural thrill of your touch vibrated even through the senseless wood into my heart—while you moved thus restlessly about the room—as if a deep sorrow or a most pronounced joy haunted your bosom—my brain reeled beneath the intoxicating spell of your presence, and it was with no merely human senses that I either saw or heard you. It was my soul only that distinguished you there....

Let me quote to you a passage from your letter:—"Although my reverence for your intellect and my admiration for your genius make me feel like a child in your presence you are not perhaps aware that I am many years older than yourself."... But grant that what you urge were even true. Do you not feel in your inmost heart of hearts that the "Soul love" of which the world speaks so often and so idly is, in this instance, at least, but the veriest—the most absolute of realities? Do you not— I ask it of your reason, *darling*, not less than of your heart—do you not perceive that it is my diviner nature—my spiritual being which burns and pants to commingle with your own? Has the soul age, Helen? Can Immortality regard Time? Can that which began never and shall never end consider a few wretched years of its incarnate life? Ah, I could *almost* be angry with you for the unwarranted wrong you offer to the sacred reality of my affection.

And how *am* I to answer what you say of your personal appearance? Have I not *seen* you, Helen? Have I not heard the more than melody of your voice? Has not my heart ceased to throb beneath the magic of your smile? Have I not held your hand in mine and looked steadily into your soul through the crystal Heaven of your eyes? Have I done all these things?—Or do I dream?—Or am I mad?

Were you indeed all that your fancy, enfeebled and perverted by illness, tempts you suppose you are, still, life of my life! I would but love you—but worship you the more. But as it is what can I—what *am* I to say? Who ever spoke of you without emotion—without praise? Who *ever* saw you and did not love?

But now a deadly terror oppresses me; for I too clearly see that these objections, so groundless—so futile.... I tremble lest they but serve to mask others more real, and which you hesitate—perhaps in pity—to confide to me.

Alas! I too distinctly perceive, also, that in no instance you have ever permitted yourself to say that you loved me. You are aware, sweet Helen, that on my part there are insuperable reasons forbidding me to urge upon you my love. Were I not poor—had not my late errors and reckless excesses justly lowered me in the esteem of the good—were I wealthy, or could I offer you worldly honours—ah then—then—how proud would I be to persevere—to *plead* with you for your love....

Ah, Helen! my soul!—what is it that I have been saying to you?—to what madness have I been urging you?—I, who am *nothing* to you—*you* who have a dear mother and sister to be blessed by your life and love. But ah, darling! if I *seem* selfish, yet believe that I truly, *truly* love you, and that it is the most spiritual love that I speak, even if I speak it from the depths of the most passionate of hearts. Think—oh, think for *me*, Helen, and for yourself....

I would comfort you—soothe you—tranquilize you. You would rest from care—from all worldly perturbation. You would get better and finally well. And if *not*, Helen—if you *died*—then, at least, I would clasp your dear hands in death, and willingly—oh, *joyfully—joyfully* go down with you into the night of the grave.

Write soon—soon—oh, soon!—but not *much*. Do not weary or agitate yourself for *my* sake. Say to me those coveted words that would turn Earth into Heaven.

BAD
LOVE

Catherine of Aragon to Henry VIII
(ca. 1536?)

My Lord and dear Husband,

I commend me unto you. The hour of my death draweth fast on, and, my ease being such, the tender love I owe you forceth me, with a few words, to put you in remembrance of the health and safeguard of your soul, which you ought to prefer before all worldly matters, and before the care and tendering of your own body, for the which you have cast me into many miseries and yourself into many cares. For my part I do pardon you all; yes, I do wish and devoutly pray God that he will also pardon you.

For the rest I commend unto you Mary, our daughter, beseeching you to be a good father unto her, as I heretofore desired. I entreat you also on behalf of my maids, to give them marriage portions, which is not much, they being but three. For all my other servants I solicit a year's pay more than their due, lest they should be unprovided for.

Lastly, I do vow, mine eyes desire you above all things.

Dorothy Osborne to Sir William Temple
(1654)

Sir,

If you have ever loved me, do not refuse the last request I shall ever make you; 'tis to preserve yourself from the violence of your passion. Vent it all upon me; call me and think me what you please; make me, if it be possible, more wretched than I am. I'll bear it all without the least murmur. Nay, I deserve it all, for had you never seen me you had certainly been happy. 'Tis my misfortunes only that have that infectious quality as to strike at the same time me and all that's dear to me. I am the most unfortunate woman breathing, but I was never false. No; I call heaven to witness that if my life could satisfy for the least injury my fortune has done you (I cannot say 'twas I that did them you), I would lay it down with greater joy than any person ever received a crown; and if I ever forget what I owe you, or ever entertained a thought of kindness for any person in the world besides, may I live a long and miserable life. 'Tis the greatest curse I can invent; if there be a greater, may I feel it. This is all I can say. Tell me if it be possible I can do anything for you, and tell me how I may deserve your pardon for all the trouble I have given you. I would not die without it.

Thomas Otway to Elizabeth Barry
(ca. 1678?)

Could I see you without passion, or be absent from you without pain, I need not beg your pardon for thus renewing my vows, that I love you more than health, or any happiness here or hereafter. Everything you do is a new charm to me; and though I have languished for seven long years, jealously despairing, yet every minute I see you I still discover something more bewitching.

Consider how I love you. What would I not renounce or undertake for you? I must have you mine, or I am miserable; and nothing but knowing which shall be the happy hour can make the rest of my life that is to come tolerable. Give me a word or two of comfort, or resolve never to look on me more; for I cannot bear a kind look, and then a cruel repulse. *This minute my heart aches for you;* and if I cannot have a right in yours, I wish it would ache till I could complain to you no longer. Remember poor

OTWAY

William Congreve to Mrs. Arabella Hunt
(ca. 1690?)

Dear Madam,

May I presume to beg pardon for the fault I committed—so foolish a fault that it was below not only a man of sense but a man; and of which nothing could ever have made me guilty but the fury of a passion with which none but your lovely self could inspire me. May I presume to beg pardon for a fault which I can never forgive myself? To purchase that pardon what would I not endure? You shall see me prostrate before you, and use me like a slave while I kiss the dear feet that trample upon me. But if my crime be too great for forgiveness, as indeed it is very great, deny me not one dear parting look; let me see you once before I must never see you more.

Christ! I want patience to support that accursed thought, I have nothing in the world that is dear to me but you. You have made everything else indifferent; and can I resolve never to see you more? In spite of myself I must always see you. Your form is fixed by fate in my mind and is never to be remov'd. I see those lovely piercing eyes continually, I see each moment those ravishing lips which I have gazed on still with desire, and still have touch'd with transport, and at which I have so often flown with all the fury of the most violent love.

Jesus! from whence and whither am I fallen? From the hopes of blissful extasies to black despair; from the expectation of immortal transports, which none but your dear self can give me, and which none but he who loves like me could ever so much as think of, to a complication of cruel passions and the most dreadful condition of human life!

My fault indeed has been very great, and cries aloud for the severest vengeance. See it inflicted on me: see me despair and die for that fault. But let me not die unpardon'd, madam; I die for you, but die in the most cruel and dreadful manner. The wretch that lies broken on the wheel alive feels not a quarter of what I endure. Yet boundless love has been all my crime.

Suffer me to take my eternal leave of you; when I have done that how easy will it be to bid all the rest of the world adieu!

George Farquhar to "Penelope" Oldfield (ca. 1700?)

Why should I write to my dearest Penelope when I only trouble her with reading what she won't believe? I have told my passion, my eyes have spoke it, my tongue pronounced it, and my pen declared it; I have sighed it, swore it, and subscribed it. Now my heart is full of you, my head raves of you, and my hand writes to you: but all in vain.

If you think me a dissembler, use me generously like a villain, and discard me forever; but if you will be so just to my passion as to believe it sincere, tell me so and make me happy: 'tis but justice, madam, to do one or t' other.

Your indisposition last night, when I left you, put me into such disorder that, not finding a coach, I missed my way and never minded where I wandered till I found myself close by *Tyburn*. When blind love guides, who can forbear going astray? Instead of laughing at myself, I fell to pitying poor Mr. F——r, who whilst he roved abroad among your whole sex was never out of his way; and now by a single she was led to the gallows. From the thought of hanging I was led to that of matrimony. I considered how many gentlemen have taken a handsome swing to avoid some inward disquiets; then why should not I hazard the noose to ease me of my torment? Then I considered whether I should send for the ordinary of *Newgate*, or the parson of St. Ann's; but, considering myself better prepared for dying in a fair lady's arms than on the three-legged tree, I was the most inclined to a parish priest. Besides, if I died in a fair lady's arms, I should be sure of Christian burial at last, and should have the most beautiful tomb in the universe.

You may imagine, madam, that these thoughts of mortality were very melancholy, but who could avoid the thought of his own death, when you were sick? And if your health be not dearer to me than my own, may the next news I hear be your death, which would be as great a hell as your life and welfare is a heaven to the most devoted of his sex.

David Hume to Madame de Boufflers
(ca. 1764?)

I could never yet accuse myself, dear madam, of hypocrisy or dissimulation; and I was surely guilty of these vices in the highest degree, if I wrote you a letter which carried with it any marks of indifference. What I said in particular I cannot entirely recollect, but I well remember in general what I felt, which was a great regard and attachment to you, not increased indeed (for that was scarce possible), but rendered more agreeable to myself, from the marks you had given me of your friendship and confidence. I adhere to these. I will never but with my life be persuaded to part the hold which you have been pleased to afford me. You may cut me to pieces, limb by limb; but like those pertinacious animals of my country, I shall expire still attached to you, and you will in vain attempt to get free.

For this reason, madam, I set at defiance all those menaces, which you obliquely throw out against me. Do you seriously think, that it is at present in your power to determine whether I shall be your friend or not? In everything else your authority over me is without control. But with all your ingenuity, you will scarce contrive to use me so ill, that I shall not still better bear it; and after all, you will find yourself obliged, from pity, or generosity, or friendship, to take me back into your service.

At least this will probably be the case, till you find one who loves you more sincerely and values you more highly; which with all your merit, I fancy it will not be easy for you to do. I know, that I am here furnishing you with arms against myself, you may be tempted to tyrannise over me, in order to try how far I will practise my doctrine of passive obedience, but I hope also that you will hold this soliloquy to yourself:—

"This poor fellow, I see is resolved never to leave me; let me take compassion on him; and endeavour to render our intercourse as agreeable to him and as little burdensome to myself as possible." If you fall, madam, into this way of thinking, as you must at last, I ask no farther; and all your menaces will vanish into smoke.

Good God! how much have I fallen from the airs which I at first gave myself? You may remember, that a little after our personal acquaintance, I told you, that you was obliged *à soutenir la gageure*, and could not in decency find fault with me, however I should think proper to behave myself. Now I throw myself at your feet, and give you nothing but marks of patience and long-suffering and submission. But I own, that matters are at present upon a more proper and more natural footing; and long may they remain so.

Julia de L'Espinesse to M. de Guibert
(ca. 1773?)

I could not write to you myself. If you love me, this will make you unhappy; and I shall be miserable at giving you pain, which I might avoid. I was in such a state of anguish it was quite agonizing. I cried bitterly for four hours. No, never did my heart suffer such utter despair. The fear of something terrible almost drives me crazy. I dread Wednesday, and it seems to me that death itself is not remedy sufficient for the loss I dread. I feel it only too much; it requires no courage to die, but it is terrible to live. I cannot endure the thought that he whom I love, and who loves me, would not hear me, nor come to my assistance. He would be horrified to see me dead. He said to me, *the 10th.* I have that within me which will make you forget all I have caused you to suffer; and this very day this sad accident befalls me!

Ah, you who have felt passion and despair, can you imagine my misfortune? Endure me while I live; but beware of ever regretting this most unhappy creature, who has existed for eight days in a state of unimaginable grief. Adieu! If I must live, if my doom is not pronounced, I shall yet find some happiness and consolation in your friendship. Will you always be my friend?

Napoleon Bonaparte to His Wife, Josephine
(1796)

For a month I have only received from my dear love two letters of three lines each. Is she so busy that writing to her dear love is not needful for her, nor, consequently, thinking about him? To live without thinking of Josephine would be death and annihilation to your husband. Your image gilds my fancies, and enlivens the black and sombre picture of melancholy and grief. A day perhaps may come when I shall see you, for I doubt not you will be still at Paris, and verily on that day I will show you my pockets stuffed with letters that I have not sent you because they are too foolish. Yes, that's the word. Good God! tell me, you who know so well how to make others love you without being in love yourself, do you know how to cure me of love? I will give a good price for that remedy....

Every day I count up your misdeeds. I lash myself to fury in order to love you no more. Bah, don't I love you the more? In fact, my peerless little woman, I will tell you my secret. Set me at defiance, stay in Paris, have lovers, let everybody know it, never write me a single syllable! Then I shall love you ten times more for it! It is folly, a delirious fever! And I shall not get the better of it. Oh, would to heaven I could recover! But don't tell me you are ill, don't try to justify yourself. Good heavens! you are pardoned. I love you to distraction, and never will my poor heart cease to give all for love. If you did not love me, my fate would be indeed grotesque....

Laurence Sterne to Elizabeth Lumley
(ca. 1839?)

You bid me tell you, my dear L——, how I bore your departure from S——, and whether the valley where D'Estella stands retains still its looks: or, if I think the roses or jessamines smell as sweet as when you left it. Alas! everything has now lost its relish and look! The hour you left D'Estella, I took to my bed. I was worn out with fevers of all kinds, but most by that fever of the heart with which thou knowest well I have been wasting these two years—and shall continue wasting till you quit S——. The good Miss S——, from the forebodings of the best of hearts, thinking I was ill, insisted upon my going to her.

What can be the cause, my dear L——, that I never have been able to see the face of this mutual friend but I feel myself rent to pieces? She made me stay an hour with her, and in that short space I burst into tears a dozen different times, and in such affectionate gusts of passion that she was constrained to leave the room, and sympathise in her dressing-room. I have been weeping for you both, said she, in a tone of the sweetest pity—for poor L's heart, I have long known it—her anguish is as sharp as yours, her heart as tender, her constancy as great, her virtues as heroic. Heaven brought you not together to be tormented. I could only answer her with a kind look and a heavy sigh, and returned home to your lodgings (which I have hired till your return) to resign myself to misery. Fanny had prepared me a supper—she is all attention to me—but I sat over it with tears; a bitter sauce, my L——, but I could eat it with no other, for the moment she began to spread my little table my heart fainted within me. One solitary plate, one knife, one fork, one glass. I gave a thousand pensive penetrating looks at the chair thou hast so often graced in those quiet and sentimental repasts, then laid down my knife and fork and took out my handkerchief, and clapped it across my face and wept like a child. I do so this very moment, my L——, for as I take up my pen my poor pulse quickens, my pale face glows, and tears are trickling down upon the paper as I trace the word L——.

Oh, thou! blessed in thyself and in thy virtues—blessed to all who know thee—to me most so, because more do I know of thee than all thy sex: this is the philtre, my L——, by which thou hast charmed me, and by which thou wilt hold me thine whilst virtue and faith hold this world together, this, my friend, is the plain and simple magic by which I told Miss —— I have won a place in that heart of thine, on which I depend so satisfied, that time, or distance, or change of everything which might alarm the hearts of little men, create no uneasy suspense in mine. Wast thou to stay in S—— these seven years, thy friend, though he would grieve, scorns to doubt, or to be doubted—'tis the only exception where security is not the parent of danger.

I told you poor Fanny was all attention to me since your departure—contrives every day bringing in the name of L——. She told me last night (upon giving me some hartshorn) she had observed my illness began the very day of your departure for S——, that I had never held up my head, had seldom, or scarce ever smiled; had fled from all society; that she verily believed I was broken-hearted, for she had never entered the room, or passed by the door, but she heard me sigh heavily; that I neither ate, or slept, or took pleasure in anything as before. Judge then my L——, can the valley look so well, or the roses and jessamines smell so sweet as heretofore? Ah me! But adieu, the vesper bell calls me from thee to my God!

L. Sterne

George Sand to Alfred de Musset
(ca. 1834?)

Why did we part so sadly? Shall we see each other tonight? Can we be happy? Can we love? You have said yes, and I have tried to believe so, but it seems to me that there is little sequence in your ideas, and that at the least thing you turn upon me as against a yoke. Alas! my child, we love, that is the only thing that we can be sure of. Time and absence have not prevented it, and will never prevent it. But is it possible for us to live together? Ought my existence to be linked with another's? The question frightens me. I am sad, or disturbed, by turns. Every moment you bring me hope and despair.

What shall I do? Do you want me to go away? Do you want to try again to forget me? As for me, I do not seek to, but I can be silent, and go away. I feel that I shall love you again as before if I do not run away. Possibly I shall kill you and myself with you. Do you think that would be nice? I want to tell you in advance all that is to be feared in our relations. I ought to have written to you that I would not come back. Fate made me come. Must we accuse her or bless her? For some hours, I must confess my terror was stronger than my love, and I felt paralysed, like a man on a mountain path between two gulfs, who dares neither to go on nor turn back. Love with you and an agonised existence for us both, perhaps, or solitude and despair for me alone. Tell me, do you not believe that you could be happy otherwise? Undoubtedly you could. You are twenty-three, and the most beautiful and the best woman in the world might belong to you. As for me, I only bring you very little happiness and a great deal of harm. It is a sorry dowry that I have for you.

Send me away, my child; say the word. This time you need fear no violence on my part, and I will ask you to render an account of the happiness which I have renounced. Tell me that you wish it, show me that you wish it. Do not think of me. I will live for you just as long as you like, and the day when you wish it to stop I will depart without ceasing to cherish you or pray for you. Consult your heart, your mind, your future, your mother; think what you have besides me, and do not sacrifice anything for me. Still, if you come back I can promise you one thing, and that is that I shall try to make you happy; but you must have patience and indulgence for those moments of fear and sadness which I may possibly go through. Patience, I know, one rarely has at your age. Think it over, my angel. My life belongs to you, and whatever happens, know that I love thee and shall love thee.

Honoré de Balzac to Madame Hanska
(Countess Evelina Rzewuska)
(1845)

I can assure you, without vanity, that my conduct is irreproachable. I rise every night. I think of you. I write to you. And I go on thus for two hours, before I am able to set to work. I continue to write, but it is to you, and not, as I ought to write, to the public; or if, by a wonderful chance, I should not think of you, then it is about one of the houses which people offer to let me, about the furniture, about its arrangement, about the thousand details of my transactions, since each matter of a thousand francs requires as much care and trouble as if it were a matter of a hundred thousand. Then I read your dear letters over again; I stare at my proofs; I scold myself. Day breaks, with nothing done. I tell myself that I am a monster, that to become worthy of you I ought to forget you, and to gird myself with the toiler's girdle. I say a thousand bitter things to myself, and I take up Daffinger's ivory. I fancy it is you in the flesh, and I dream, and I awake in despair to find that I have been dreaming instead of working.

LOVE
ON THE
ROCKS

James, Lord of Chanvallon, to Margaret of Valois
(ca.1580?)

⁓⁓

You are pleased, my Queen, to accuse me of infidelity, although you cannot doubt what I am to you any more than you can be ignorant of what you are to me, although I resent the cruelty of your extreme commands, the which I judge as obnoxious to myself as they are unworthy of you, since they prevent me from bearing testimony to my infinite love.

If from such things you have until now drawn cause to torture and sacrifice me, and to extract the quintessence of what reposes in my heart and soul, now, with so many just and obvious reasons, you ought to recognise that I am all yours. Have the good will to recognise that if you wish me not to resent the injury to my faith and patience, you should, at least, recompense me by ceasing those insupportable torments with which you have afflicted me, ever since your perfections rendered me their slave. Remember, my Queen, those holy vows of yesterday, which I renewed in your beautiful hands, and you must admit the sincerity of my devotion, and the more so because you know all that I said to you was not the least evidence of my affection.

I know that it may seem strange to you that I dare most humbly to beg the honour of a quarter-hour's talk with you tomorrow. But I learned something today which you ought to know, but which is of such a kind that it does not lend itself to writing, as you can yourself judge. One of my friends told me that you showed yourself ill satisfied with me. You know, madam, whether you have cause, since you only appreciate the effects of my violent passion. So have pity on me and on my heart, and vouchsafe to suffer for him who loves you so slight an inconvenience. Most humbly do I kiss your beautiful hands.

Henry of Navarre to Henrietta D'Entragues
(1608)

It does not appear who deprives you of news of me, but the experiences of five years have forced me into the belief that you love me not. During that time your actions have been so contrary to your words and writing and to the love you owe me that at length your ingratitude has overturned a passion which resisted longer than any did before.

Remembering how much suffering I have endured by it, if you have yet a scrap of affection left, with it you should have some regret. I hold one thing with God: conversion, not death. It was for you to speak French down yonder, for I always hear that language willingly, as it is mine from choice. If you have the devil in you, wait where you are; if some good little devil possesses you, come to Marcoussis, which, being nearer, the truth will reveal itself the better.

Ebba Brahe to Gustavus Adolphus
(1618)

Most Gracious, Illustrious Master,
  Friend, and King,
  Her Majesty the Queen compelleth me to wed Count Jacob de la Gardie at the palace next Sunday. Have pity upon me, your Majesty, and save me from this horror. You know full well how I devoted my heart to you when you plighted me your heart's troth. If your Majesty come not in your own person to my relief, then must I relinquish all hope of

another happy hour during this my earthly term. Come to the aid of your dear Ebba, who loves your Majesty unto pallid death.

George Farquhar to "Penelope" Oldfield
(ca. 1700?)

Madam,

'Tis a sad misfortune to begin a letter with an *adieu*; but when my love is crossed, 'tis no wonder that my writing should be reversed. I would beg your pardon for the other offences of this nature which I have committed, but that I have so little reason to judge favourably of your mercy; though I can assure you, Madam, that I shall never excuse myself my own share of the trouble, no more than I can pardon myself the vanity of attempting your charms, so much above the reach of my pretensions, and which are reserved for some more worthy admirer. If there be that man upon earth that can merit your esteem, I pity him,—for an obligation too great for a return must, to any generous soul, be very uneasy,—though I still envy his misery.

May you be as happy, Madam, in the enjoyment of your desires as I am miserable in the disappointment of mine; and, as the greatest blessing of your life, may the person you most admire love you as sincerely and as passionately as he whom you scorn.

FARQUHAR

Lady Mary Pierrepont to Edward Wortley Montagu
(1711)

I intended to make no answer to your letter; it was something very ungrateful, and I resolved to give over all thoughts of you. I could easily have performed that resolve some time ago, but then you took pains to please me; now you have brought me to esteem you, you make use of that esteem to give me uneasiness; and I have the displeasure of seeing I esteem a man that dislikes me. Farewell then: since you will have it so, I renounce all the ideas I have so long flattered myself with, and will entertain my fancy no longer with the imaginary pleasure of seeing you.

I fondly thought fine clothes and gilt coaches, balls, operas, and public adoration, rather the fatigues of life; and that true happiness was justly defined by Mr. Dryden (pardon the romantic air of repeating verses) when he says,

> Whom Heav'n would bless it does from pomps remove,
> And makes their wealth in privacy and love.

According to this scheme I proposed to pass my life with you. I yet do you the justice to believe, if any man could have been contented with this manner of living it would have been you.

Your indifference to me does not hinder me from thinking you capable of tenderness, and the happiness of friendship, but I find it is not to me you'll ever have them. You think me all that is detestable; you accuse me of want of sincerity and generosity. To convince you of your mistake I'll show you the last extremes of both.

While I foolishly fancied you loved me, (which I confess I had never any great reason for, more than that I wished it) there is no condition of life I could not have been happy in with you, so very much I liked you—

I may say loved, since it is the last thing I'll ever say to you. This is telling you sincerely my greatest weakness; and now I will oblige you with a new proof of generosity—I'll never see you more. I shall avoid all public places; and this is the last letter I shall send. If you write be not displeased if I send it back unopened. I shall force my inclinations to oblige yours; and remember that you have told me I could not oblige you more than by refusing you. Had I intended ever to see you again, I durst not have sent this letter. Adieu.

Samuel Johnson to Mrs. Thrale
(1784)

Dear Madam,

What you have done, however I may lament it, I have no pretence to resent, as it has not been injurious to me; I, therefore, breathe out one sigh more of tenderness, perhaps useless, but at least sincere.

I wish that God may grant you every blessing, that you may be happy in this world for its short continuance, and eternally happy in a better state; and whatever I can contribute to your happiness I am very ready to repay, for the kindness which soothed twenty years of a life radically wretched.

Do not think slightly of the advice which I now presume to offer. Prevail upon Mr. Piozzi to settle in England; you may live here with more dignity than in Italy, and with more security: your rank will be higher, and your fortune more under your own eye. I desire not to detail my reasons; but even argument of prudence and interest is for England, and only some phantoms of imagination seduce you to Italy.

I am afraid, however, that my counsel is vain, yet I have eased my heart by giving it.

When Queen Mary took the resolution of sheltering herself in England, the Archbishop of St. Andrew's, attempting to dissuade her, attended her on her journey, and when they came to that irremeable stream that separated the two kingdoms, walked by her side into the water, in the middle of which he seized her bridle, and with earnestness proportioned to her own danger and his own affection pressed her to return. The queen went forward. If the parallel reaches thus far, may it go no farther—the tears stand in my eyes.

I am going into Derbyshire, and hope to be followed by your good wishes, for I am, with great affection,

Yours, &c.,

SAMUEL JOHNSON

Mary Wollstonecraft to Captain Gilbert Imlay (1795)

I have only to lament that, when the bitterness of death was past, I was inhumanly brought back to life and misery. But a fixed determination is not to be baffled by disappointment; nor will I allow that to be a frantic attempt which was one of the calmest acts of reason. In this respect I am only accountable to myself. Did I care for what is termed reputation, it is by other circumstances that I should be dishonoured.

You say, "that you know not how to extricate ourselves out of the wretchedness into which we have been plunged." You are extricated long since. But I forbear to comment. If I am condemned to live longer, it is a living death.

It appears to me that you lay much more stress on delicacy than on principle; for I am unable to discover what sentiment of delicacy would have been violated by your visiting a wretched friend, if indeed you have any friendship for me. But since your new attachment is the only sacred thing in your eyes, I am silent—. Be happy! My complaints shall never more damp your enjoyment; perhaps I am mistaken in supposing that even my death could for more than a moment. This is what you call magnanimity. It is happy for yourself that you possess this quality in the highest degree.

Your continually asserting that you will do all in your power to contribute to my comfort, when you only allude to pecuniary assistance, appears to me a flagrant breach of delicacy. I want not such vulgar comfort, nor will I accept it. I never wanted but your heart. That gone, you have nothing more to give. Had I only poverty to fear, I should not shrink from life. Forgive me then, if I say that I shall consider any direct or indirect attempt to supply my necessities as an insult which I have not merited, and as rather done out of tenderness for your own reputation than for me. Do not mistake me; I do not think that you value money, therefore I will not accept what you do not care for, though I do much less, because certain privations are not painful to me. When I am dead, respect for yourself will make you take care of the child.

I write with difficulty—probably I shall never write to you again. Adieu. God bless you!

Napoleon Bonaparte to His Ex-wife, Josephine (1810)

My Dear,

I have yours of April 19th; it is written in a bad style. I am always the same; people like me do not change. I know not what Eugene has told you. I have not written to you because you have not written to me, and my sole desire is to fulfil your slightest inclination.

I see with pleasure that you are going to Malmaison, and that you are contented; as for me, I shall be so likewise on hearing news from you, and in giving you mine. I say no more about it until you have compared this letter with yours, and after that I will leave you to judge which of us two is the better friend.

Goodbye, dear. Keep well, and be just for your sake and mine.

NAPOLEON

Josephine to Her Ex-husband, Napoleon Bonaparte (1810)

A thousand, thousand loving thanks for not having forgotten me. My son has just brought me your letter. With what passion I read it! And yet I took a long time over it, for there was not a word which did not make me weep; but these tears were very soothing. I have found my whole heart again—such as it will always be; there are affections which are life itself, and which can only end with it.

I was in despair to find my letter of the 19th had displeased you; I do not remember the exact expression, but I know what torture I felt in writing it—the grief at having no news from you.

I wrote you on my departure from Malmaison, and since then how often have I wished to write you! But I appreciated the causes of your silence, and feared to be importunate with a letter. Yours has been true balm for me. Be happy, be as much so as you deserve; it is my whole heart which speaks to you. You have also just given me my share of happiness, and a share which I value the most, for in my estimation nothing can equal a proof that you still remember me.

Adieu, dear. I again thank you as affectionately as I shall always love you.

JOSEPHINE

Lord Byron to Lady Byron
(1816)

All I can say seems useless—and all I could say might be no less unavailing—yet I still cling to the wreck of my hopes, before they sink for ever. Were you, then, *never* happy with me? Did you never at any time or times express yourself so? Have no marks of affection of the warmest and most reciprocal attachment passed between us? or did in fact hardly a day go down without some such on one side, and generally on both? Do not mistake me: I have not denied my state of mind—but you know its causes—and were those deviations from calmness never followed by acknowledgments and repentance? Was not the last that recurred more particularly so? and had I not—had we not the days before and on the day we parted—every reason to believe that we loved each other? that we were to meet again? Were not your letters kind? Had I not acknowledged to you all my faults and follies—and assured you that some had not and could not be repeated? I do not require these questions to be answered to me, but to your own heart....

Upon your letter to me this day I surely may remark that its expressions imply a treatment which I am incapable of inflicting, and you of imputing to me, if aware of their latitude, and the extent of the inference to be drawn from them. This is not just, but I have no reproaches nor the wish to find cause for them. Will you see me ?—when and where you please—in whose presence you please. The interview shall pledge you to nothing, and I will say and do nothing to agitate either. It is torture to correspond thus, and there are things to be settled and said which cannot be written.

William Hazlitt to Sarah Walker
(1822)

When I think of the thousand endearing caresses that have passed between us, I do not wonder at the strong attachment that draws me to you; but I am sorry for my own want of power to please. I hear the wind sigh through the lattice, and keep repeating over and over to myself two lines of Lord Byron's tragedy:

> So shalt thou find me ever at thy side.
> Here and hereafter, if the last may be.

applying them to thee, my love, and thinking whether I shall ever see thee again. Perhaps not—for some years at least—till both thou and I are old—and then, when all else have forsaken thee, I will creep to thee, and die in thine arms. You once made me believe I was not hated by her I loved; and for that sensation, so delicious was it, though but a mockery and a dream, I owe you more than I can ever pay. I thought to have dried up my tears for ever, the day I left you; but as I write this, they stream again. If they did not, I think my heart would burst. I walk out here of an afternoon, and hear the notes of the thrush, that comes up from a sheltered valley below, welcome in the spring; but they do not melt my heart as they used; it is grown cold and dead. As you say it will one day be colder.—Forgive what I have written above; I did not intend it; but you were once my little all, and I cannot bear the thought of having lost you forever, I fear through my own fault. . . . Kiss me my best beloved. Ah! if you can never be mine, still let me be your proud and happy slave.

H.

THE WORLD'S
GREATEST
LOVER

The Love Letters of John Keats
to Fanny Brawne

T he letters that John Keats wrote to Fanny Brawne feature some of the most eloquent expressions of love ever committed to paper. When Keats met Brawne in 1818, at the age of twenty-three, he was already regarded a promising young poet. In the years that their romance flourished, Keats was to write poems that are now regarded masterpieces of English literature, among them "Ode on a Grecian Urn," "The Even of St. Agnes," "La Belle Dame sans Merci," and "Hyperion." Keats's love for Fanny undoubtedly influenced his masterful verse—just as his awareness of his imminent death shaped the emotions that he expressed in his letters to her. Shortly before he made Fanny's acquaintance, Keats developed symptoms of tuberculosis, the disease that would eventually take his life. He wrote regularly to Fanny up until September 1820, when he departed for Italy and a climate that he hoped would help him overcome his illness. Yet both knew they likely would never see each other again. Keats died in Rome on February 23, 1821.

John Keats to Fanny Brawne
(1819)

My dearest Lady,

I am glad I had not an opportunity of sending off a letter which I wrote for you on Tuesday night—'twas too much like one out of Rousseau's "Héloïse." I am more reasonable this morning. The morning is the only proper time for me to write to a beautiful girl whom I love so much: for at night, when the lonely day has closed, and the lonely, silent, unmusical Chamber is waiting to receive me as into a sepulchre, then believe me my passion gets entirely the sway, then I would not have you see those rhapsodies which I once thought it impossible I should ever give way to, and which I have often laughed at in another, for fear you should (think me) either too unhappy or perhaps a little mad.

I am now at a very pleasant cottage window, looking onto a beautiful hilly country, with a glimpse of the sea; the morning is very fine. I do not know how elastic my spirit might be, what pleasure I might have in living here and breathing and wandering as free as a stag about this beautiful coast if the remembrance of you did not weigh so upon me. I have never known any unalloyed happiness for many days together: the death or sickness of some one has always spoiled my hours—and now when none such troubles oppress me, it is, you must confess, very hard that another sort of pain should haunt me. Ask yourself, my love, whether you are not very cruel to have so entrammelled me, so destroyed my freedom. Will you confess this in the letter you must write immediately, and do all you can to console me in it—make it rich as a draught of poppies to intoxicate me—write the softest words and kiss them that I may at least touch my lips where yours have been. For myself, I know not how to express my devotion to so fair a form: I want a brighter word than bright, a fairer word than fair. I almost wish we were butterflies and lived but three summer days—three such days with you I could fill with more delight than fifty common years could ever contain.

I am sure I could never act selfishly: as I told you a day or two before I left Hampstead, I will never return to London if my Fate does not turn up Pam or at least a Court-card. Though I could centre my happiness in you, I cannot expect to engross your heart so entirely—indeed if I thought you felt as much for me as I do for you at this moment, I do not think I could restrain myself from seeing you again tomorrow for the delight of one embrace. But no—I must live upon hope and Chance. In case of the worst that can happen, I shall still love you—but what hatred shall I have for another! Some lines I read the other day are continually ringing a peal in my ears:

> To see those eyes I prize above mine own
> Dart favours on another—
> And those sweet lips (yielding immortal nectar)
> Be gently pressed by any but myself—
> Think, think, Francesca, what a cursed thing
> It were beyond expression!

Do write immediately. There is no post from this place, so you must address Post Office, Newport, Isle of Wight. I know before night I shall curse myself for having sent you so cold a letter; yet it is better to do it as much in my senses as possible. Be as kind as the distance will permit to your

J. KEATS

Present my compliments to your mother, my love to Margaret and best remembrances to your brother—if you please so.

John Keats to Fanny Brawne
(1819)

My Sweet Girl,

Your letter gave me more delight than anything in the world but yourself could do; indeed, I am almost astonished that any absent one should have that luxurious power over my senses which I feel. Even when I am not thinking of you I receive your influence and a tenderer nature stealing upon me. All my thoughts, my unhappiest days and nights, have, I find, not at all cured me of my love of Beauty, but made it so intense that I am miserable that you are not with me, or, rather, breathe in that dull sort of patience that cannot be called Life. I never knew before what such a love as you have made me feel was. I did not believe in it; my fancy was afraid of it, lest it should burn me up. But if you will fully love me, though there may be some fire, 'twill not be more than we can bear, when moistened and bedewed with Pleasures.

You mention "horrid people," and ask me whether it depend upon them whether I see you again. Do understand me, my love, in this. I have so much of you in my heart that I must turn Mentor when I see a chance of harm befalling you. I would never see anything but Pleasure in your eyes, love on your lips, and Happiness in your steps. I would wish to see you among those amusements suitable to your inclinations and spirits; so that our loves might be a delight in the midst of Pleasures agreeable enough, rather than a resource from vexations and cares. But I doubt much, in case of the worst, whether I shall be philosopher enough to follow my own Lessons; if I saw my resolution give you pain, I could not.

Why may I not speak of your Beauty, since without that I could never have loved you? I cannot conceive any beginning of such love as I have for you but Beauty. There may be a sort of love for which, without the least sneer at it, I have the highest respect, and can admire it in others; but it has not the richness, the bloom, the full form, the enchantment, of love after my own heart. So let me speak of your Beauty, though to my own endangering, if you could be so cruel as to try elsewhere its Power. You say you are afraid I shall think you do not love me; in saying this you make me ache the more to be near you. I am at the diligent use of my faculties here,—I do not pass a day without sprawling some blank verse or tagging some rhymes; and here I must confess that (since I am on that subject) I love you the more in that I believe that you have liked me for my own sake and for nothing else. I have met with women who I really think would like to be married to a Poem and to be given away by a Novel.

I have seen your Comet, and only wish it was a sign that poor Rice would get well, whose illness makes him rather a melancholy companion; and the more so as so to conquer his feelings and hide them from me with a forced Pun. I kissed your writing over in the hope you had indulged me by leaving a trace of honey. What was your dream? Tell it me and I will tell you the interpretation thereof. Ever yours, my love,

JOHN KEATS

John Keats to Fanny Brawne
(1819)

My dearest Girl,

This moment I have set myself to copy some verses out fair. I cannot proceed with any degree of content. I must write you a line or two, and see if that will assist in dismissing you from my Mind for ever so short a time. Upon my Soul, I can think of nothing else. The time is past when I had power to advise and warn you against the unpromising morning of my Life. My love has made me selfish. I cannot exist without you. I am forgetful of everything but seeing you again; my Life seems to stop there; I see no further. You have absorbed me. I have a sensation at the present moment as though I was dissolving: I should be exquisitely miserable without the hope of soon seeing you. I should be afraid to separate myself far from you. My sweet Fanny, will your heart never change? My love, will it? I have no limit now to my love.

Your note came in just here. I cannot be happier away from you. 'Tis richer than an argosy of pearls. Do not threat me, even in jest. I have been astonished that men could die Martyrs for religion,—I have shuddered at it. I shudder no more; I could be martyred for my Religion,—love is my religion,—I could die for that. I could die for you. My Creed is Love, and you are its only tenet. You have ravished me away by a Power I cannot resist; and yet I could resist till I saw you; and even since I have seen you I have endeavoured often "to reason against the reasons of my Love." I can do that no more,—the pain would be too great. My love is selfish. I cannot breathe without you.

Yours forever,

JOHN KEATS

John Keats to Fanny Brawne
(1820)

My dear Fanny,

Do not let your mother suppose that you hurt me by writing at night. For some reason or other your last night's note was not so treasurable as former ones. I would fain that you call me *Love* still. To see you happy and in high spirits is a great consolation to me; still let me believe that you are not half so happy as my restoration would make you. I am nervous, I own, and may think myself worse than I really am; if so, you must indulge me, and pamper with that sort of tenderness you have manifested towards me in different Letters. My sweet creature, when I look back upon the pains and torments I have suffered for you from the day I left you to go to the Isle of Wight, the ecstasies in which I have passed some days and the miseries in their turn, I wonder the more at the Beauty which has kept up the spell so fervently. When I send this round I shall be in the front parlour watching to see you show yourself for a minute in the garden. How illness stands as a barrier betwixt me and you! Even if I was well— I must make myself as good a Philosopher as possible. Now I have had opportunities of passing nights anxious and awake, I have found other thoughts intrude upon me. "If I should die," said I to myself, "I have left no immortal work behind me,—nothing to make my friends proud of my memory,—but I have loved the principle of beauty in all things, and if I had had time I would have made myself remembered." Thoughts like these came very feebly whilst I was in health, and every pulse beat for you; now you divide with this (may *I* say it?) "last infirmity of noble minds" all my reflection.

God bless you, love!

J. Keats

John Keats to Fanny Brawne
(1820)

Sweetest Fanny,

You fear sometimes I do not love you so much as you wish? My dear Girl, I love you ever and ever and without reserve. The more I have known you the more have I lov'd. In every way,—even my jealousies have been agonies of Love; in the hottest fit I ever had I would have died for you. I have vexed you too much. But for Love! Can I help it? You are always new. The last of your kisses was ever the sweetest, the last smile the brightest; the last movement the gracefullest. When you pass'd my window home yesterday, I was fill'd with as much admiration as if I had seen you for the first time. You uttered a half complaint once that I only lov'd your beauty. Have I nothing else then to love in you but that? Do I not see a heart naturally furnish'd with wings imprison itself with me? No ill prospect has been able to turn your thoughts a moment from me. This perhaps should be as much a subject of sorrow as joy—but I will not talk of that. Even if you did not love me I could not help an entire devotion to you: how much more deeply then must I feel for you knowing you love me. My Mind has been the most discontented and restless one that ever was put into a body too small for it. I never felt my Mind repose upon anything with complete and undistracted enjoyment—upon no person but you. When you are in the room my thoughts never fly out of window; you always concentrate my whole senses. The anxiety shown about our Loves in your last note is an immense pleasure to me; however, you must not suffer such speculations to molest you any more; nor will I any more believe you can have the least pique against me.

Brown is gone out, but here is Mrs. Wylie; when she is gone I shall be awake for you. Remembrances to your Mother.

Your affectionate,

J. KEATS

John Keats to Fanny Brawne
(1820)

My dearest Girl,

I have been a walk this morning with a book in my hand, but as usual I have been occupied with nothing but you; I wish I could say in an agreeable manner. I am tormented day and night. They talk of my going to Italy. 'Tis certain I shall never recover if I am to be so long separate from you; yet with all this devotion to you I cannot persuade myself into any confidence of you.

Past experience connected with the fact of my long separation from you gives me agonies which are scarcely to be talked off. When your mother comes I shall be very sudden and expert in asking her whether you have been to Mrs. Dilke's, for she might say no to make me easy.

I am literally worn to death, which seems my only recourse. I cannot forget what has pass'd. What? Nothing with a man of the world, but to me deathful. I will get rid of this as much as possible. When you were in the habit of flirting with Brown you would have left off, could your own heart have felt one half of the one pang mine did. Brown is a good sort of Man—he did not know he was doing me to death by inches. I feel the effect of every one of those hours in my side now; and for that cause, though he has done me many services, though I know his love and friendship for me, though at this moment I should be without pence were it not for his assistance, I will never see or speak to him until we are both old men, if we are to be.

I *will* resent my heart having been made a football. You will call this madness. I have heard you say that it was not unpleasant to wait a few years, you have amusements—your mind is away—you have not brooded over one idea as I have, and how should you? You are to me an object intensely desirable—the air I breathe in a room empty of you is unhealthy. I am not the same to you—no—you can wait—you have a thousand activities—you can be happy without me. Any party, anything to fill up the day has been enough.

How have you passed this month? Who have you smil'd with? All this may seem savage in me. You do not feel as I do, you do not know what it is to love, one day you may, your time is not come. Ask yourself how many unhappy hours Keats has caused you in Loneliness. For myself I have been a Martyr the whole time, and for this reason I speak; the confession is forc'd from me by the torture. I appeal to you by the blood of that Christ you believe in: Do not write to me if you have done anything this month which it would have pained me to have seen. You may have altered—if you have not—if you still behave in dancing rooms and other societies as I have seen you—I do not want to live—if you have done so, I wish this coming night may be my last.

I cannot live without you, and not only you but *chaste you, virtuous you*. The Sun rises and sets, the day passes, and you follow the bent of your inclination to a certain extent, you have no conception of the quantity of miserable feeling that passes through me in a day.

Be serious! Love is not a plaything—and again do not write unless you can do it with a crystal conscience. I would sooner die for want of you than ——

Yours for ever,

J. KEATS

John Keats to Fanny Brawne
(1820)

My Dearest Fanny,

My head is puzzled this morning, and I scarce know what I shall say, though I am full of a hundred things. 'Tis certain I would rather be writing to you this morning, notwithstanding the alloy of grief in such an occupation, than enjoy any other pleasure, with health to boot, unconnected with you.

Upon my soul I have loved you to the extreme. I wish you could know the Tenderness with which I continually brood over your different aspects of countenance, action and dress. I see you come down in the morning: I see you meet me at the Window: I see everything over again eternally, that I ever have seen. If I get on the pleasant clue, I live in a sort of happy misery, if on the unpleasant 'tis miserable misery.

You complain of my ill-treating you in word, thought, and deed—I am sorry,—at times I feel bitterly sorry that I ever made you unhappy—my excuse is that those words have been wrung from me by the sharpness of my feelings. At all events and in any case I have been wrong; could I believe that I did it without any cause, I should be the most sincere of Penitents. I could give way to my repentant feelings now, I could recant all my suspicions, I could mingle with you heart and Soul, though absent, were it not for some parts of your Letters.

Do you suppose it possible I could ever leave you? You know what I think of myself and what of you. You know that I should feel how much it was my loss and how little yours. My friends laugh at you! I know some of them—when I know them all I shall never think of them again as friends or even acquaintances.

My friends have behaved well to me in every instance but one, and there they have become tattlers and inquisitors into my conduct: spying upon a secret I would rather die than share it with anybody's confidence. For this I cannot wish them well, I care not to see any of them again. If I am the Theme, I will not be the Friend of idle Gossips.

Good gods! what a shame it is our Loves should be so put into the microscope of a Coterie! Their laughs should not affect you (I may perhaps give you reasons some day for these laughs, for I suspect a few people to hate me well enough, *for reasons I know of*, who have pretended a great friendship for me) when in competition with one, who, if he should never see you again would make you the Saint of his memory.

These Laughers who do not like you, who envy you for your Beauty, who would have God-bless'd me from you for ever; who were plying me with disencouragements with respect to you eternally.

People are revengeful—do not mind them—do nothing but love me— if I knew that for certain life and health will in such event be a heaven, and death itself will be less painful. I long to believe in immortality— I shall never be able to bid you an entire farewell.

If I am destined to be happy with you here—how short is the longest Life. I wish to believe in immortality—I wish to live with you for ever. Do not let my name ever pass between you and these laughers; if I have no other merit than the great Love for you, that were sufficient to keep me sacred and unmentioned in such society.

If I have been cruel and unjust, I swear my love has ever been greater than my cruelty, which lasts but a minute, whereas my Love, come what will, shall last for ever.

If concession to me has hurt your Pride God knows I have had little pride in my heart when thinking of you. Your name never passes my Lips — do not let mine pass yours. Those people do not like me. After reading my Letter you even then wish to see me. I am strong enough to walk over— but I dare not. I shall feel so much pain in parting with you again.

My dearest love, I am afraid to see you; I am strong, but not strong enough to see you. Will my arm be ever round you again, and if so shall I be obliged to leave you again?

My sweet love! I am happy whilst I believe your first Letter. Let me be but certain that you are mine heart and soul, and I could die more happily than I could otherwise live.

If you think me cruel—if you think I have sleighted you—do muse it over again and see into my heart. My love to you is true as truth's simplicity and simpler than the infancy of truth, as I think I once said before. How could I slight you? How threaten to leave you? Not in the spirit of a threat to you—no—but in the spirit of Wretchedness in myself.

My fairest, my delicious, my angel Fanny! do not believe me such a vulgar fellow. I will be as patient in illness and as believing in Love as I am able.

Yours forever, my dearest,

JOHN KEATS

John Keats to Fanny Brawne
(1820)

My dearest Girl,

I wish you could invent some means to make me at all happy without you. Every hour I am more and more concentrated in you; everything else tastes like chaff in my Mouth.

I feel it almost impossible to go to Italy—the fact is I cannot leave you, and shall never taste one minute's content until it pleases chance to let me live with you for good. But I will not go on at this rate. A person in health as you are can have no conception of the horrors that nerves and a temper like mine go through. What Island do your friends propose retiring to?

I should be happy to go with you there alone, but in company I should object to it; the back-bitings and jealousies of new colonists who have nothing else to amuse themselves, is unbearable. Mr. Dilke came to see me yesterday, and gave me a very great deal more pain than pleasure. I shall never be able any more to endure the society of any of those who used to meet at Elm Cottage and Wentworth Place. The last two years taste like brass upon my Palate.

If I cannot live with you I will live alone. I do not think my health will improve much while I am separated from you. For all this, I am averse to seeing you. I cannot bear flashes of light, and return into my gloom again. I am not so unhappy now as I should be if I had seen you yesterday.

To be happy with you seems such an impossibility! it requires a luckier Star than mine! it will never be. I enclose a passage from one of your letters which I want you to alter a little.

I want (if you will have it so) the matter express'd less coldly to me. If my health would bear it, I could write a Poem which I have in my head, which would be a consolation for people in such a situation as mine. I would show some one in Love as I am, with a person living in such Liberty as you do.

Shakespeare always sums up matters in the most sovereign manner. Hamlet's heart was full of such Misery as mine is when he said to Ophelia, "Go to a nunnery, go, go!" Indeed I should like to give up the matter at once.

I should like to die. I am sickened at the brute world which you are smiling with. I hate men, and women more. I see nothing but thorns for the future—wherever I may be next winter, in Italy or nowhere, Brown will be living near you with his indecencies.

I see no prospect of any rest. Suppose me in Rome— well, I should there see you as in a magic glass, going to and from town at all hours—I wish you could infuse a little confidence of human nature into my heart. I cannot muster any—the world is too brutal for me. I am glad there is such a thing as the grave—I am sure I never shall have any rest till I get there. At any rate I will indulge myself by never seeing any more Dilke or Brown, or any of their Friends.

I wish I was either in your arms full of faith or that a Thunder bolt would strike me. God bless you.

J.K.

John Keats to Charles Armitage Brown
(1820)

My Dear Brown:

Saturday we were let out of quarantine, during which my health suffered more from bad air and the stifled cabin than it had done the whole voyage. The fresh air revived me a little, and I hope I am well enough this morning to write you a short, calm letter—if that may be called one in which I am afraid to speak of what I would fainest dwell upon. As I have gone thus far into it, I must go on a little; perhaps it will relieve the load of wretchedness that presses upon me. The persuasion that I shall see her no more will kill me. My dear Brown, I should have had her when I was in health, and I should have remained well. I can bear to die—I cannot bear to leave her. Oh God! God! God! Everything I have in my trunks that reminds me of her goes through me like a spear. The silk lining she put in my travelling cap scalds my head. My imagination is horridly vivid about her—I see her—I hear her. There is nothing in the world of sufficient interest to divert me from her for a moment. This was the case when I was in England: I cannot recollect, without shuddering, the time I was a prisoner at Hunt's, and used to keep my eyes fixed on Hampstead all day. Then there was a good hope of seeing her again. Now—O that I could be buried near where she lives! I am afraid to write to her—to receive a letter from her: to see her handwriting would break my heart—even to hear of her anyhow, to see her name written would be more than I could bear. My dear Brown, what am I to do? Where can I look for consolation or ease? If I had any chance of recovery, this passion would kill me. Indeed, through the whole of my illness, both at your house and at Kentish Town, this fever has never ceased wearing me out. When you write to me, which you will do immediately, write to Rome (*poste restante*)—if she is well and happy put a mark thus +: if— * * My dear Brown, for my sake, be her advocate for ever. I cannot say a word about Naples; I do not feel at all concerned in the thousand novelties around me; I am afraid to write to her. I should like her to know that I do not forget her. Oh! Brown, I have coals of fire in my breast: it surprises me that the human heart is capable of bearing and containing so much misery. Was I born for this end? God bless her, and her mother, and my sister, and George and his wife, and you, and all!